Rita Foelker

super
fun
food
Origami
for Kids

Happy Fox
BOOKS

Super Fun Food Origami for Kids © Snake SA 2019

This edition © 2022 Happy Fox Books, an imprint of Fox Chapel Publishing Company, Inc., 903 Square Street, Mount Joy, PA 17552.

First published in Italian in 2019 by **nuinui**® a registered trademark of Snake SA, Chemin du Tsan du Péri, 10, 3971 Chermingon, Switzerland

Editorial director: Federica Romagnoli
Editorial coordinator: Paolo Biano
Editor: Maria Pia Bellizzi
English translation: Freire Disseny + Comunicació
Graphic design: Marinella Debernardi
Graphics manager: Stefania Costanzo
Cover graphics: Marinella Debernardi
Origami sheet illustrations: Vu Kim Ngan
Illustrations: Pretty Vectors / Shutterstock.com
Web support: QL Tech s.r.l., Milan

978-1-64124-150-2

To learn more about the other great books from Fox Chapel Publishing, or to find a retailer near you, call toll-free 800-457-9112 or visit us at www.FoxChapelPublishing.com.

We are always looking for talented authors. To submit an idea, please send a brief inquiry to acquisitions@foxchapelpublishing.com

Fox Chapel Publishing makes every effort to use environmentally friendly paper for printing.

Printed in China
First printing

Scan the QR codes with a smartphone or a tablet using the camera or a QR scanning application to access the videos.

To access the video tutorials for all the projects, visit: www.nuinui.ch/it/libro/origamoni-il-piccolo-chef/video

To download and print additional copies of the patterned origami papers in this book, visit: www.nuinui.ch/media/upload/origamoni-il-piccolo-chef.pdf

CENTRO DIFFUSIONE ORIGAMI
CASELLA POSTALE 28
27011 BELGIOIOSO (PAVIA)
e-mail: info@origami-cdo.it

The publisher thanks the Origami Diffusion Center for its valuable collaboration. For almost 40 years it has brought together Italian origamists and encouraged the exchange of experiences among enthusiasts. www.origami-cdo.it

TEXT AND DIAGRAMS BY
⇨ **Rita Foelker**

PHOTOGRAPHY BY
⇨ **Dario Canova**

VIDEOS BY {
Gemma Turnone
(origami artist)

Paolo Biano
(production)

contents

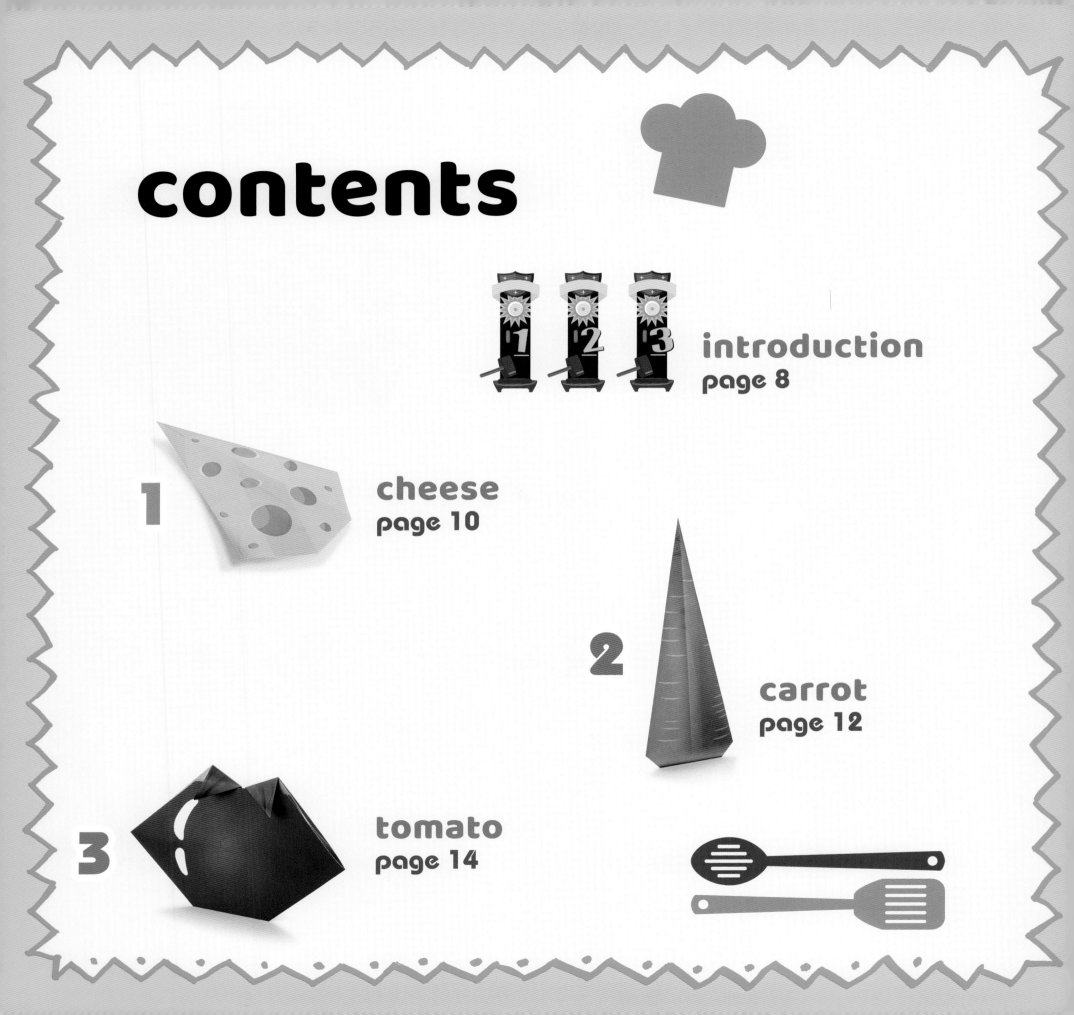

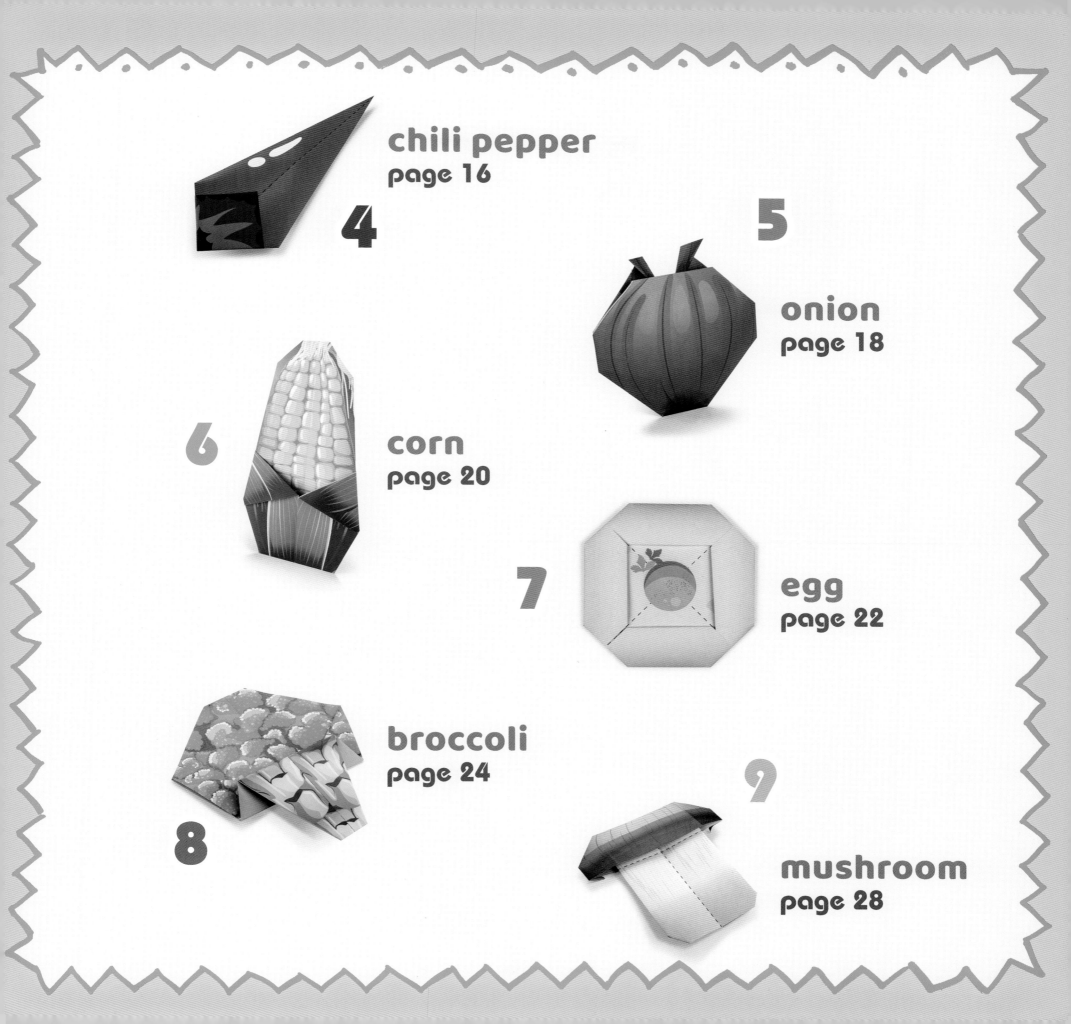

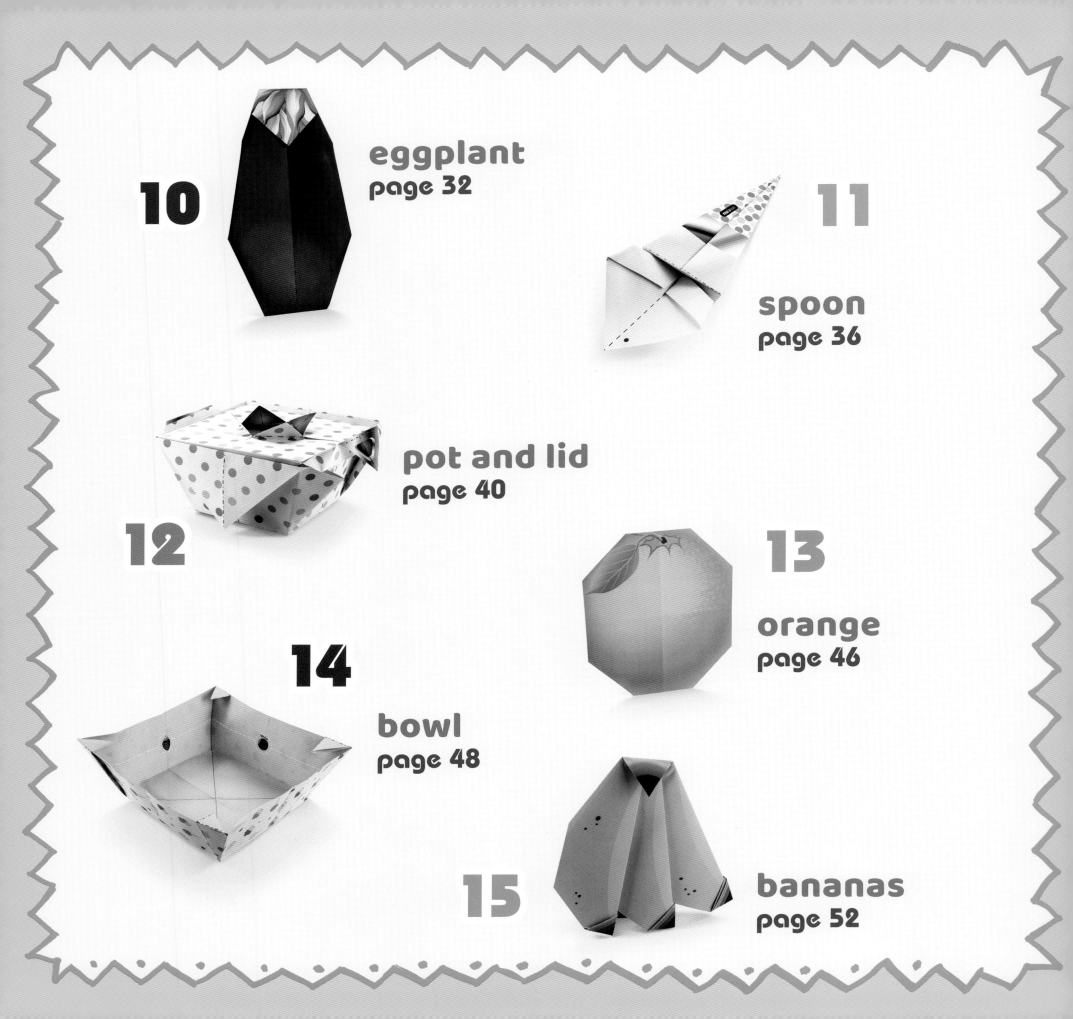

introduction

Sometimes, when I'm not folding origami, I go into the kitchen to make delicious meals. We all need to eat, of course, because **we all need nutrients**—vitamins, proteins, carbohydrates, minerals, and other substances essential for life and health. It is these nutrients that give us the energy to move, play, study, and grow. Food is for nourishment, but we also eat for other reasons: to try different flavors, to taste dishes from different countries and cultures, and, most importantly, because **food is delicious!** The discovery of great combinations of flavors is now a popular art form all over the world—we call it "gastronomy," and it includes drinks as well as food.

A tip for parents: If your child is very young, help them by folding and unfolding the project yourself first. This way, your child won't have to pay close attention to exact fold lines and will finish folding their origami in the blink of an eye. Work on a smooth, hard surface, and don't forget good lighting.

Food has a profound **emotional relationship** with the culture of every location and the people who live there, not just because of the way it is produced and cooked, but also because of how it is eaten. Preparing mouthwatering food is a way to share important moments with friends and family, like when we celebrate birthdays and weddings. People who cook love to **exchange recipes** with others and learn new and different ways to prepare meals, then share their dishes as a **gesture of love, friendship, and kindness.** In this book, I want to introduce you to a set of origami projects representing various foods and kitchen items. As you begin to fold, you will enter a colorful, delicious, and nutritious universe!

Thanks to the folding done by a talented young origamist—someone who folds origami!—there is a **video tutorial** (available by link or QR code) for every single project in this book. These videos are a wonderful tool to allow children to understand and easily follow each folding step.

types of folds

On each of the sheets provided, the folds are already marked. A dashed black line means **fold forward**, the easiest and most natural fold, where you bring the edges of the paper up toward yourself. A red line with alternating dashes and dots means **fold to the back side**, where you fold the edges of the paper down away from yourself. I tried not to use too many folds like this, since they're a little less instinctual for children.

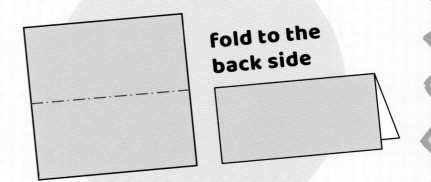

fold to the back side

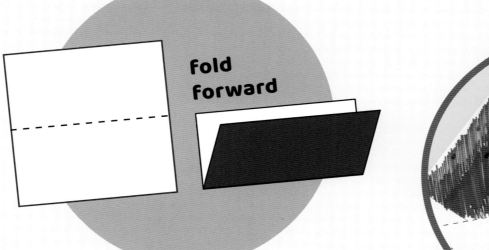

fold forward

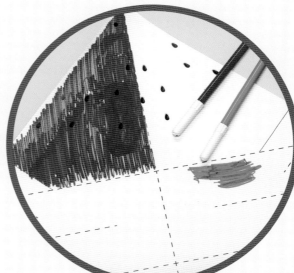

how to orient the paper

Before beginning to fold any project, you have to correctly orient the paper. On the sheets provided for each project, **a small black dot** indicates the side to place facing up before starting to fold, as well as the edge or angle that should be at the top once the paper is placed on the work surface. (It's not always the illustrated side that starts face up—it's often the back side of the paper!)

VIDEO: www.nuinui.ch/it/libro/origamoni-il-piccolo-chef/video/786

⇧ Sheets included

1 cheese

Cheese is one of the most popular dairy products eaten today. Whether the milk comes from **cows, goats, or sheep**, there is a huge variety of cheeses and there are many different ways to eat cheese. History tells us that the **ancient Egyptians** were the first to domesticate animals and that milk and cheese were an important part of their civilization. Since then, by adding different **salts and spices** or by changing the ripening time and other factors, many different types of cheese have been developed. Milk in its natural state does not last very long before it spoils, so cheese, which remains fresh much longer than milk, has become a way to store milk for a long time, retaining its nutrients.

DIFFICULTY

1

1
FOLD IN HALF ALONG THE VERTICAL DIAGONAL LINE, THEN UNFOLD.

2
FOLD THE SIDES IN TO MEET THE CENTER LINE.

4

YOUR SLICE OF CHEESE IS
READY FOR YOU TO TAKE A
(PLAY) BITE!

3

FOLD THE TOP CORNER
DOWN. FLIP THE PIECE OVER.

VIDEO: www.nuinui.ch/it/libro/origamoni-il-piccolo-chef/video/787

⇧ Sheets included

2 carrot

They say that **rabbits** like to eat carrots, which are one of their favorite foods. It was Bugs Bunny who started this legend. In real life, however, rabbits like grass and hay more than they like carrots! For us humans, eating carrots is very important. Their orange color tells us that they are rich in **beta-carotene**, which is very good for the **immune system** and helps us resist disease.

1

FOLD IN HALF ALONG THE VERTICAL DIAGONAL LINE, THEN UNFOLD.

DIFFICULTY 1

2

FOLD THE SIDES IN TO MEET THE CENTER LINE.

3

FOLD THE SIDES IN AGAIN TO MEET
THE CENTER LINE.

4

FOLD THE TOP CORNER
DOWN. FLIP THE PIECE OVER.

5

MAKE SURE A BUNNY DOES NOT
STEAL YOUR CARROT!

VIDEO: www.nuinui.ch/it/libro/origamoni-il-piccolo-chef/video/788

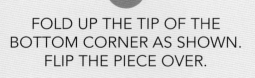

⇧ Sheets included

3 tomato

Tomatoes are wonderful. They start out **small and green**, but over time they become **red and ripe**. They are one of the main ingredients in many delicious **Italian sauces**, such as Bolognese sauce. They are also delicious in salads or on **pizza**—and you can't make **ketchup** without tomatoes!

1
FOLD IN HALF ALONG THE HORIZONTAL DIAGONAL LINE.

2
FIRST FOLD THE TOP CORNER DOWN, THEN FOLD THE SIDE CORNERS INTO THE CENTER.

3
FOLD UP THE TIP OF THE BOTTOM CORNER AS SHOWN. FLIP THE PIECE OVER.

5

YOUR RIPE, TASTY TOMATO IS READY!

4

FOLD DOWN THE TWO TOP FLAPS TO FORM TWO SMALL LEAVES.

DIFFICULTY

1

⇧ Sheets included

4 chili pepper

Chili peppers are actually the **berries** of some varieties of plants. They are used as a spice and to flavor food. They are among the most popular condiments in the world. **Before 1492**, they were present only in the Americas, but after the discovery of the American continents, chili peppers began to be transported by ship, originally by the Portuguese and Spaniards, to Europe, Asia, and Africa. All peppers have a **spicy taste**—some are **mild**, and some are **very hot**. If you want to try a spicy dish, be sure to remember to be careful about the quantity of chili pepper you add to the recipe!

1

FOLD IN HALF ALONG THE VERTICAL DIAGONAL LINE, THEN UNFOLD.

2

FOLD THE TOP CORNER DOWN.

3

FLIP THE PIECE OVER.

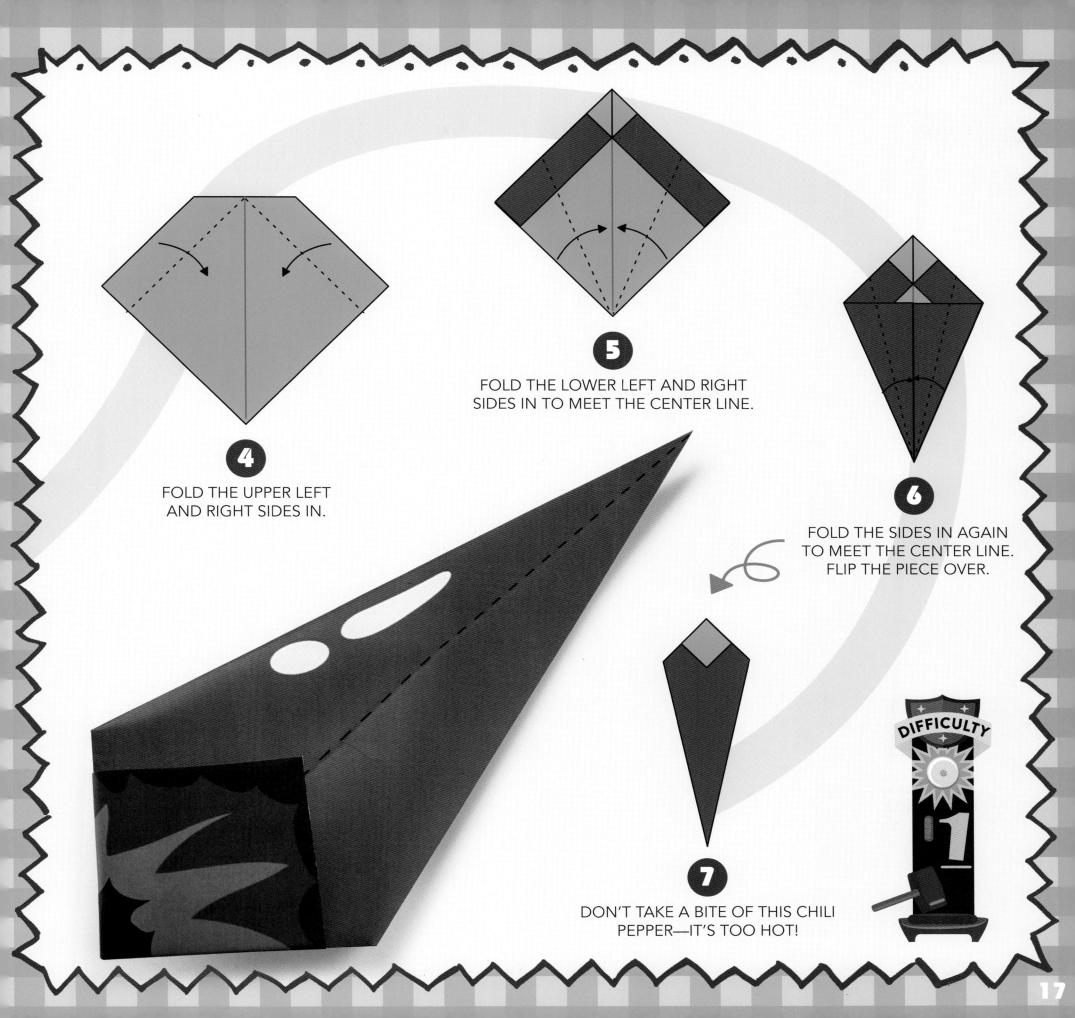

4

FOLD THE UPPER LEFT
AND RIGHT SIDES IN.

5

FOLD THE LOWER LEFT AND RIGHT
SIDES IN TO MEET THE CENTER LINE.

6

FOLD THE SIDES IN AGAIN
TO MEET THE CENTER LINE.
FLIP THE PIECE OVER.

7

DON'T TAKE A BITE OF THIS CHILI
PEPPER—IT'S TOO HOT!

DIFFICULTY

1

⇧ Sheets included

5 onion

The onion is a plant whose **bulb** is eaten all over the world. Because of its strong flavor, it makes a very popular condiment. Onion soup is a well-known dish in German and French cuisine, while breaded and **fried onion rings** are very popular in many restaurants. In many cultures, the onion is thought to have **therapeutic properties** and may be helpful in treating various health problems.

1

FOLD IN HALF ALONG THE DIAGONAL LINES, THEN UNFOLD. THEN FOLD IN HALF UPWARD.

DIFFICULTY

1

2

FOLD THE TOP CORNER DOWN. FOLD EACH OF THE SIDE CORNERS UP AT THE ANGLE SHOWN.

5

HERE'S YOUR ONION! DON'T SLICE IT, OR IT MIGHT MAKE YOU CRY!

4

FOLD EACH OF THE SIDE CORNERS IN. FOLD THE BOTTOM CORNER TO THE BACK SIDE. FLIP THE PIECE OVER.

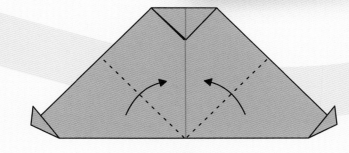

3

FOLD EACH HALF IN TO MEET THE CENTER LINE.

⇧ Sheets included

corn

Corn is one of the **most popular grains in the world** and is considered one of the most nutritious foods available. This means it contains high-power nutrients, which can help fight hunger and give you energy. It can also be used to produce **candies, cookies, bread, chocolates, pastries**—and even **popcorn!** But keep in mind that the corn used to make popcorn is different from normal corn that you would eat cooked.

1

FOLD IN HALF ALONG THE VERTICAL DIAGONAL LINE, THEN UNFOLD.

DIFFICULTY

2

2

FOLD THE SIDES IN TO MEET THE CENTER LINE.

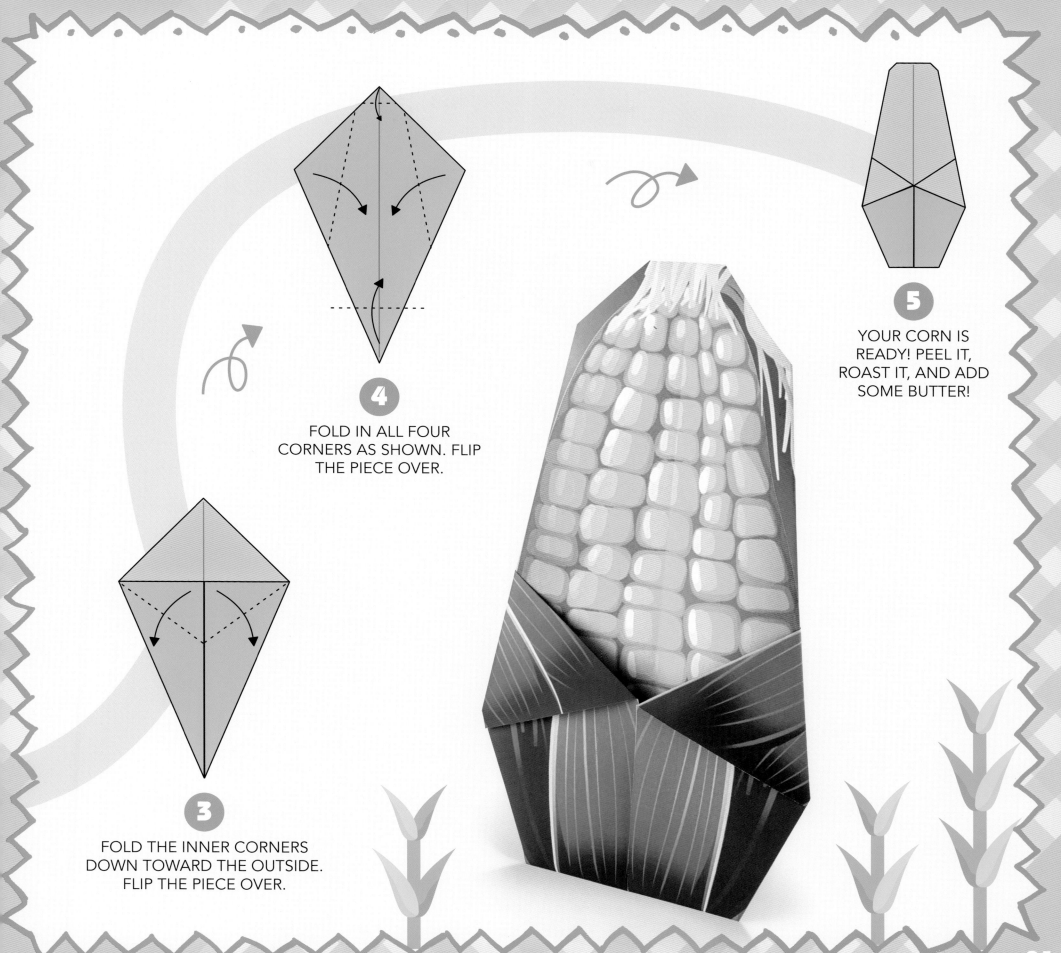

4

FOLD IN ALL FOUR
CORNERS AS SHOWN. FLIP
THE PIECE OVER.

5

YOUR CORN IS
READY! PEEL IT,
ROAST IT, AND ADD
SOME BUTTER!

3

FOLD THE INNER CORNERS
DOWN TOWARD THE OUTSIDE.
FLIP THE PIECE OVER.

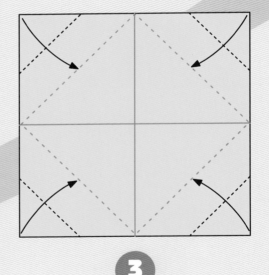

⇧ Sheets included

7 egg

Eggs are fundamental foods in many cultures. **Chicken eggs** are the most common and well-known, but people also eat quail eggs and even ostrich eggs. They can be boiled, fried, or cooked into **omelets**, and they are also used in recipes for bread, cakes, desserts, and many other preparations. It is not advisable to eat **raw eggs** due to bacteria such as salmonella that can be found in them. This bacteria can cause serious diseases, but it is destroyed by heat during cooking.

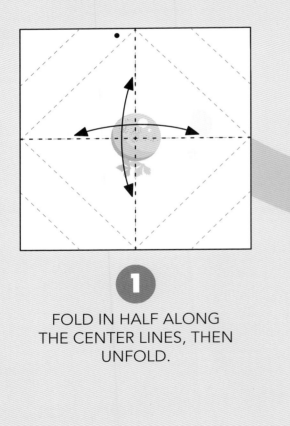

1

FOLD IN HALF ALONG THE CENTER LINES, THEN UNFOLD.

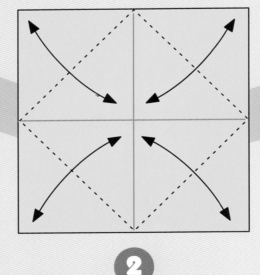

2

FOLD EACH OF THE CORNERS INTO THE CENTER, THEN UNFOLD.

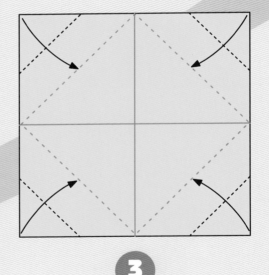

3

NOW FOLD A PART OF EACH CORNER TOWARD THE CENTER AS SHOWN.

4

FOLD THE FOUR SIDES IN AGAIN, REUSING THE FOLD YOU ALREADY CREATED.

5

FOLD EACH OF THE FOUR CORNERS TO THE BACK SIDE.

DIFFICULTY 2

6

HERE'S YOUR FRIED EGG, SUNNY-SIDE UP!

23

VIDEO: www.nuinui.ch/it/libro/origamoni-il-piccolo-chef/video/793

⇧ Sheets included

8 broccoli

Broccoli has been grown since the age of the **Roman Empire** and is still eaten today in many parts of the world. You can prepare broccoli in many ways, such as **raw, pickled, steamed, fried, and breaded**. It is also used in recipes for soups, creams, and salads. Even pizza with broccoli is delicious!

1

FOLD IN HALF ALONG THE VERTICAL DIAGONAL LINE, THEN UNFOLD.

DIFFICULTY 2

2

FOLD THE SIDES IN TO MEET THE CENTER LINE.

3

FOLD THE INNER
CORNERS DOWN
TOWARD THE OUTSIDE.

4

FIRST FOLD THE BOTTOM
CORNER TO THE BACK SIDE AS
SHOWN, THEN FOLD THE ENTIRE
BOTTOM HALF UP TO CREATE
ONE ZIGZAG FOLD.

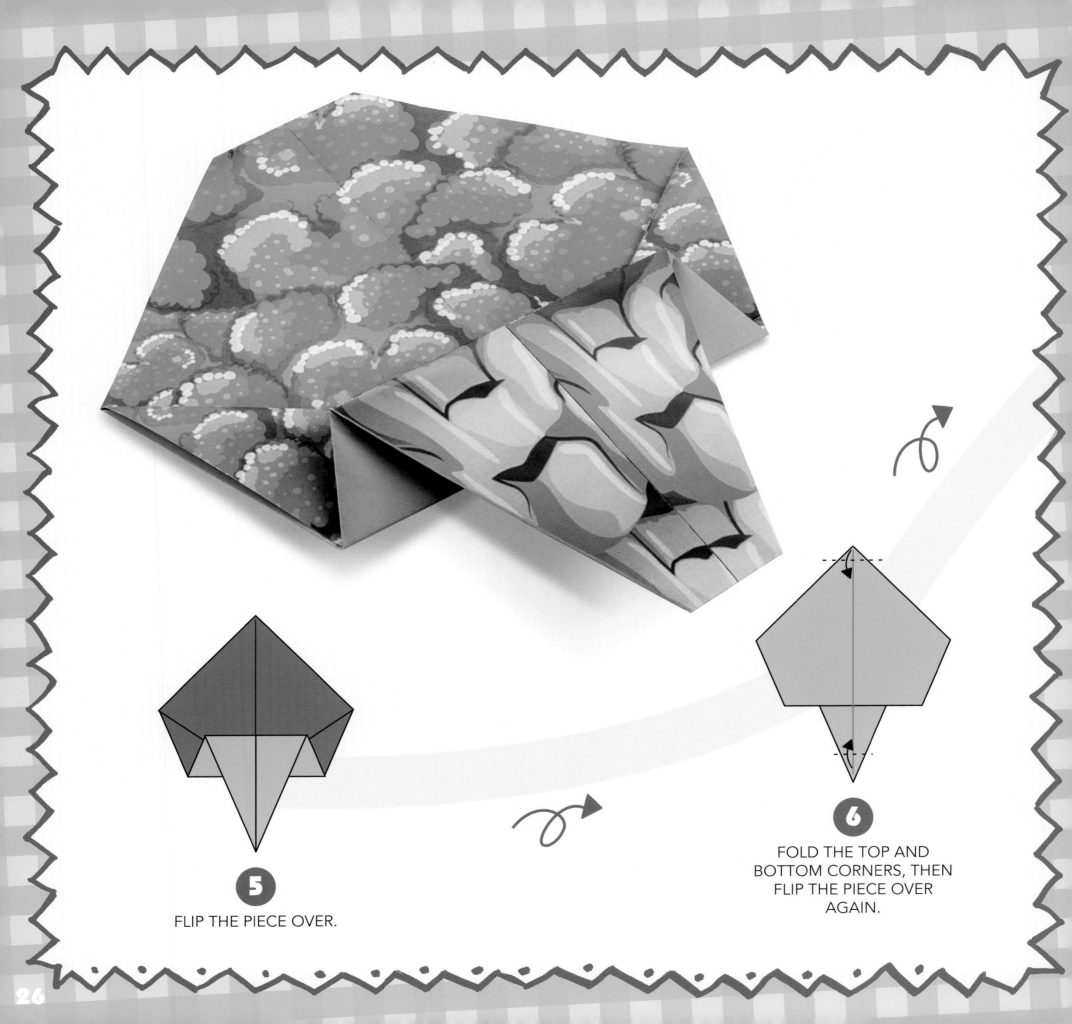

5

FLIP THE PIECE OVER.

6

FOLD THE TOP AND BOTTOM CORNERS, THEN FLIP THE PIECE OVER AGAIN.

7

BOIL THIS BROCCOLI, IT WILL BE DELICIOUS!

⬆ Sheets included

9 **mushroom**

Button mushrooms, also called white mushrooms, common mushrooms, or champignons de Paris (the capital of France), are a type of **edible mushroom**. Not all mushrooms can be eaten—many are **poisonous!** You should only eat mushrooms purchased at a store or approved by an expert. All edible mushrooms are **rich in protein and low in calories**. They are very popular in European and Asian cuisine.

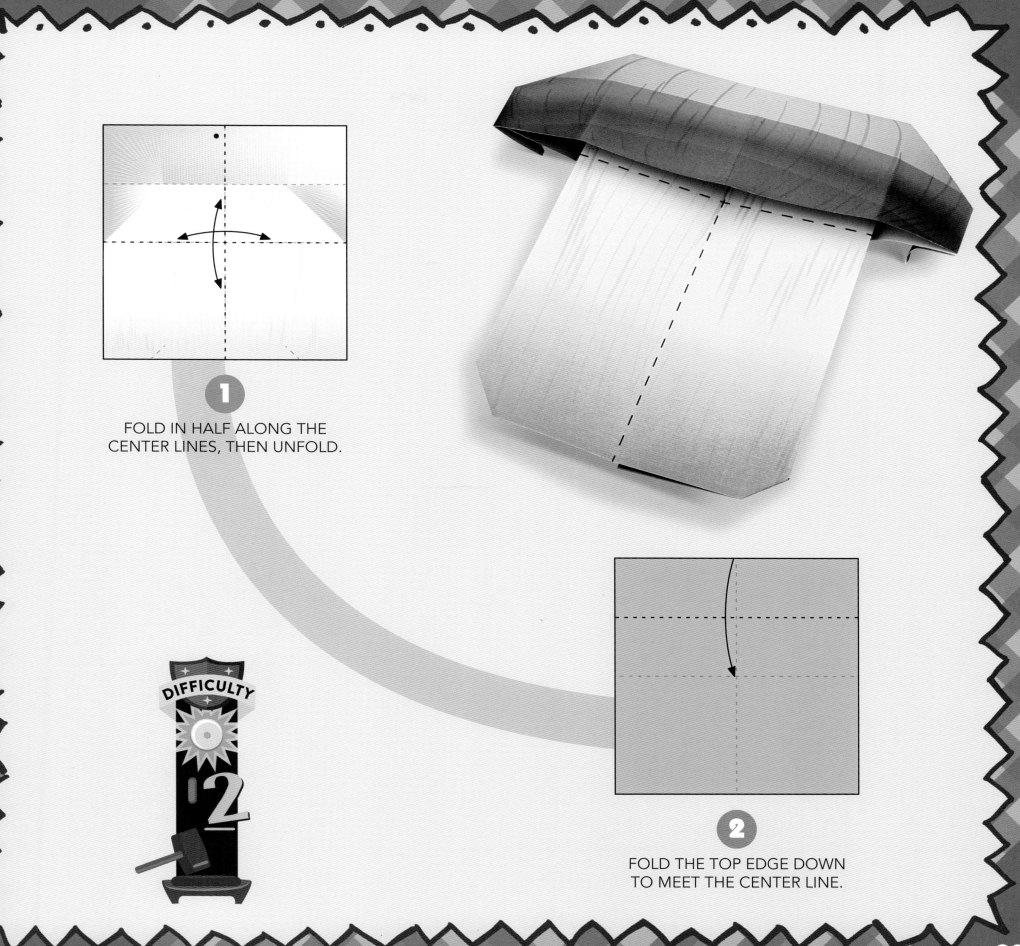

1

FOLD IN HALF ALONG THE
CENTER LINES, THEN UNFOLD.

DIFFICULTY

2

2

FOLD THE TOP EDGE DOWN
TO MEET THE CENTER LINE.

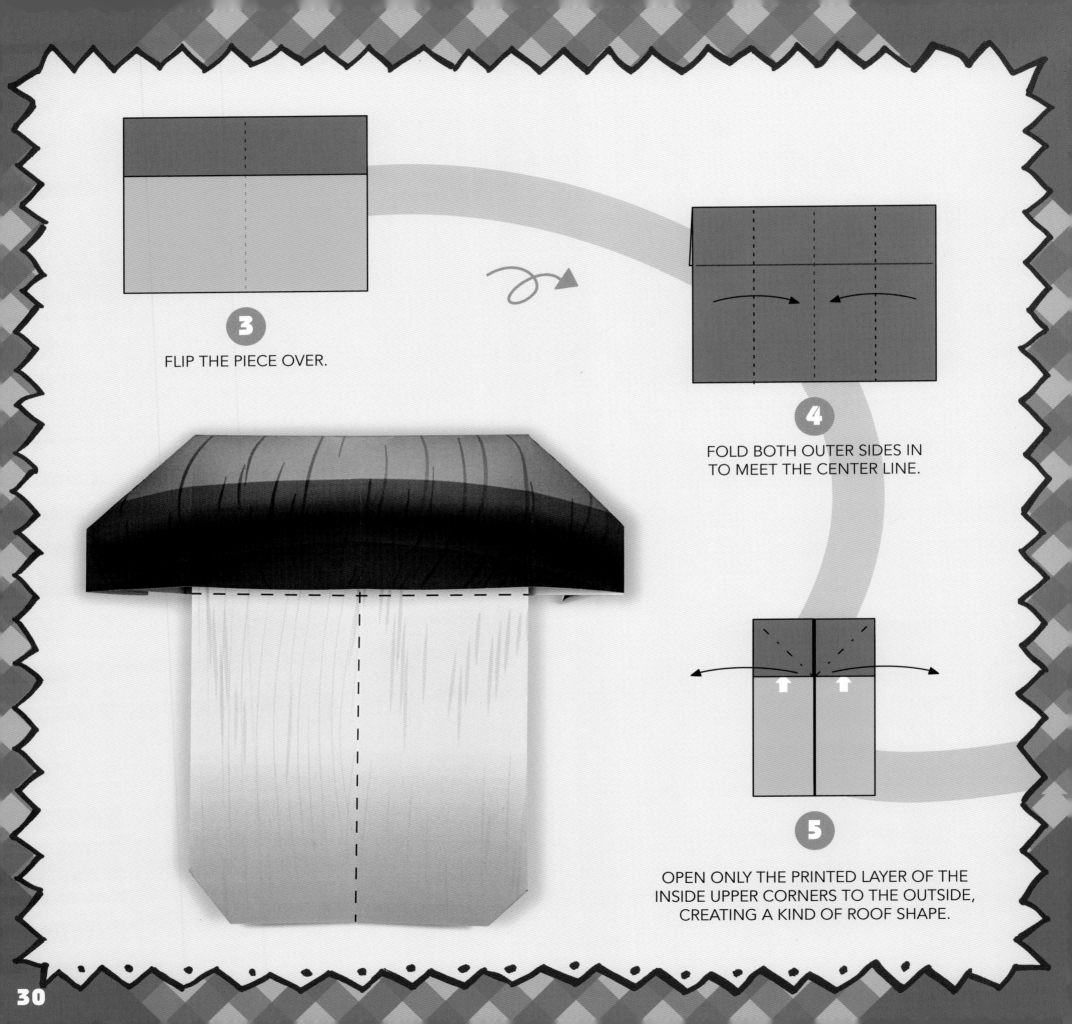

3

FLIP THE PIECE OVER.

4

FOLD BOTH OUTER SIDES IN TO MEET THE CENTER LINE.

5

OPEN ONLY THE PRINTED LAYER OF THE INSIDE UPPER CORNERS TO THE OUTSIDE, CREATING A KIND OF ROOF SHAPE.

7

WHO KNOWS IF THIS MUSHROOM IS
POISONOUS OR EDIBLE? BETTER TO
BE SAFE THAN SORRY!

6

FOLD THE FOUR CORNERS
TOWARD THE CENTER AS SHOWN.
FLIP THE PIECE OVER.

⇧ Sheets included

10 eggplant

Eggplant is beautiful to look at, but not all kids like it—or maybe not all kids have tried it! Smart people, however, **never say "I don't like it" without first having tasted something**. You can bake eggplant in the oven or fry breaded eggplant. It is also used in many delicious recipes with **pasta and cheese**.

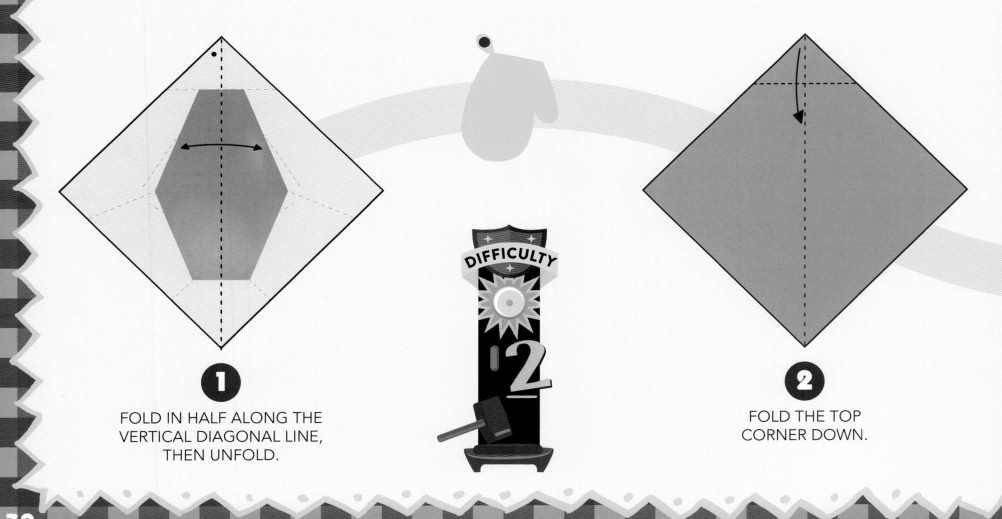

1

FOLD IN HALF ALONG THE VERTICAL DIAGONAL LINE, THEN UNFOLD.

DIFFICULTY

2

2

FOLD THE TOP CORNER DOWN.

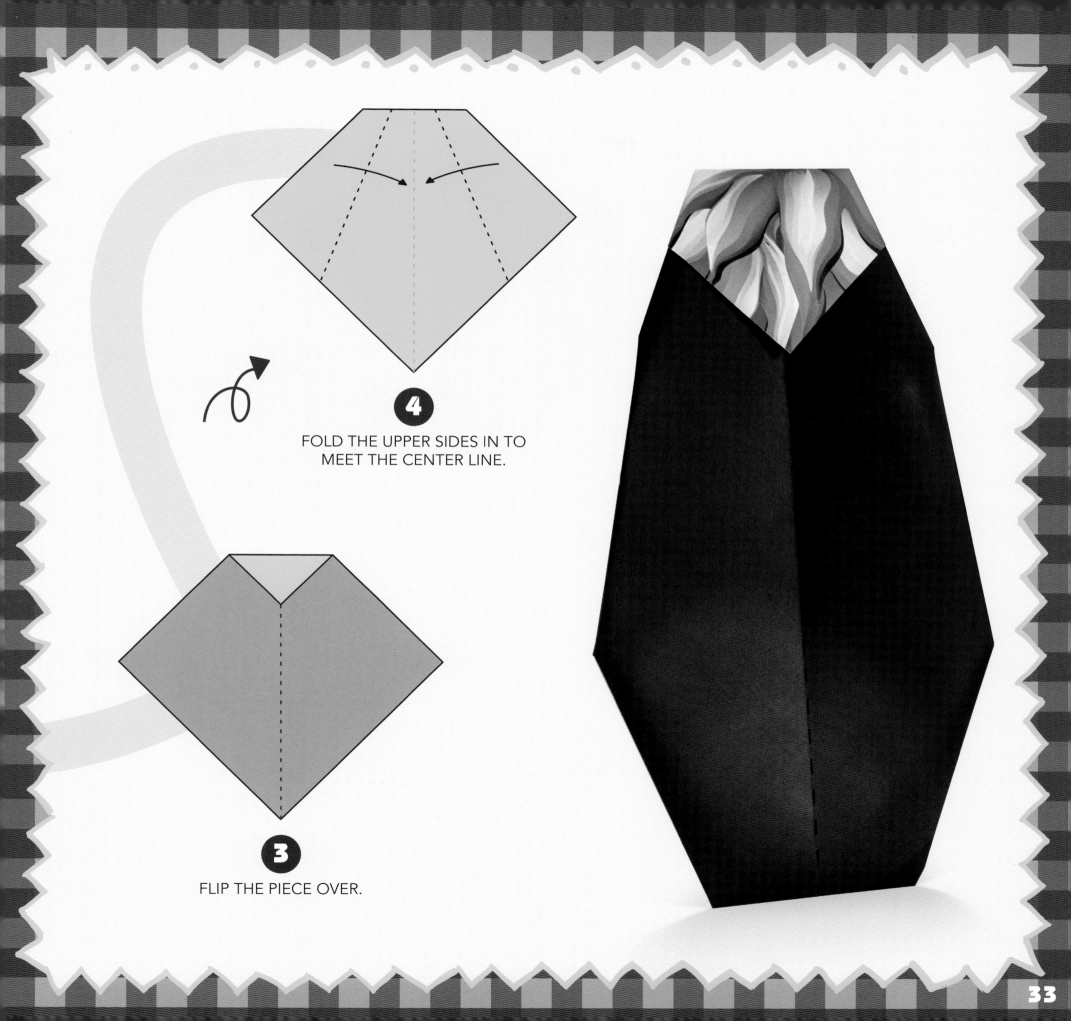

4

FOLD THE UPPER SIDES IN TO
MEET THE CENTER LINE.

3

FLIP THE PIECE OVER.

5

FOLD THE LOWER SIDES IN TO
MEET THE CENTER LINE.

6

FOLD THE THREE CORNERS SHOWN
TOWARD THE CENTER. FLIP THE
PIECE OVER.

7

YOUR EGGPLANT IS READY TO
TOSS INTO THE PAN!

⇧ Sheets included

11

spoon

The spoon is a very important tool in the kitchen. There are very large spoons and very small spoons. Some are made of stainless steel and some are made of wood or other materials. We use **large spoons** to mix food and to serve portions to different diners, **medium spoons** to eat dessert, soups, and cereal, and **tiny spoons** to add seasonings, sugar, spices, or any ingredient that needs to be added in small quantities.

1

FOLD IN HALF ALONG THE
VERTICAL DIAGONAL LINE,
THEN UNFOLD.

DIFFICULTY

3

2

FOLD THE SIDES IN TO
MEET THE CENTER LINE.

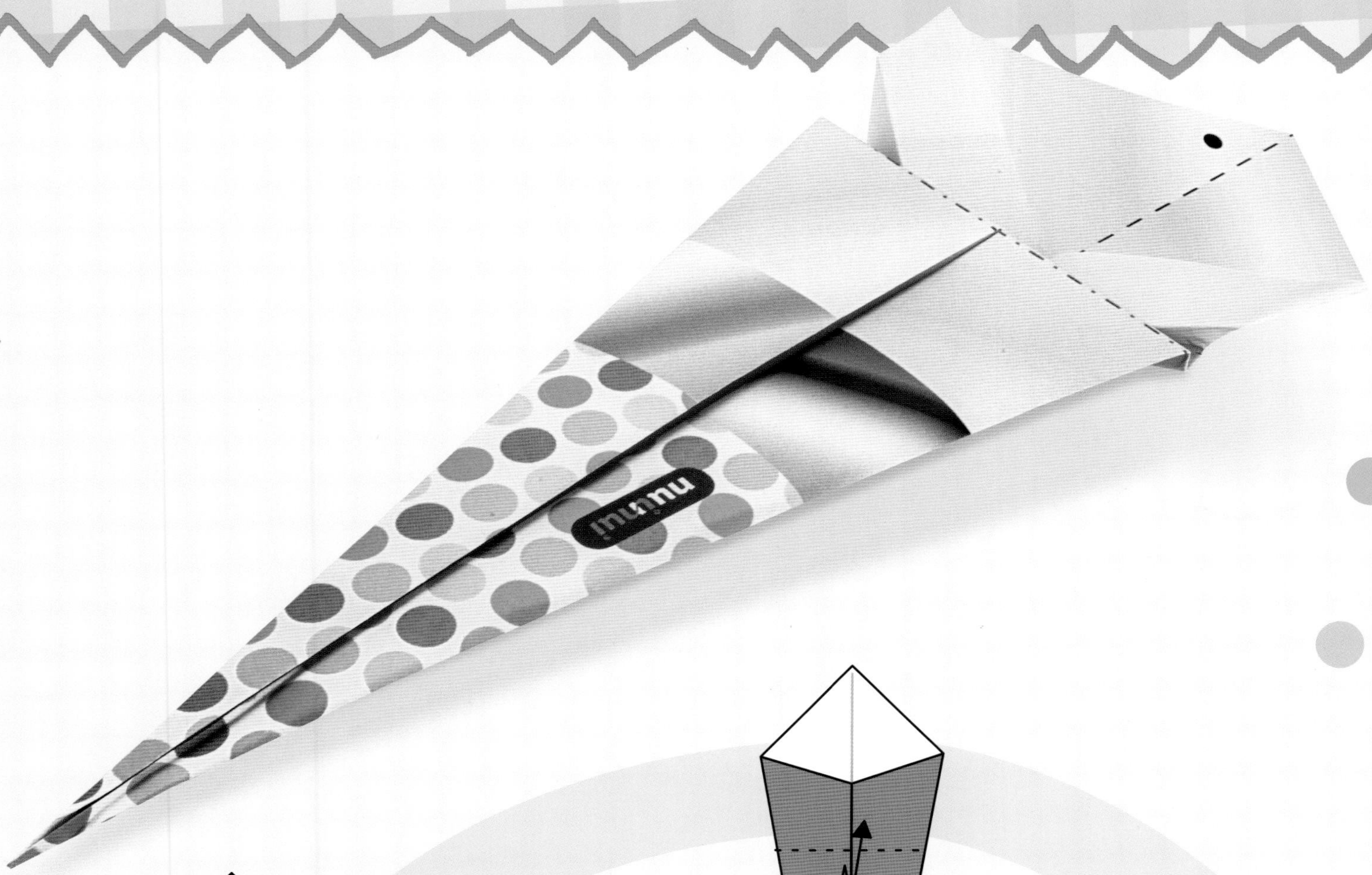

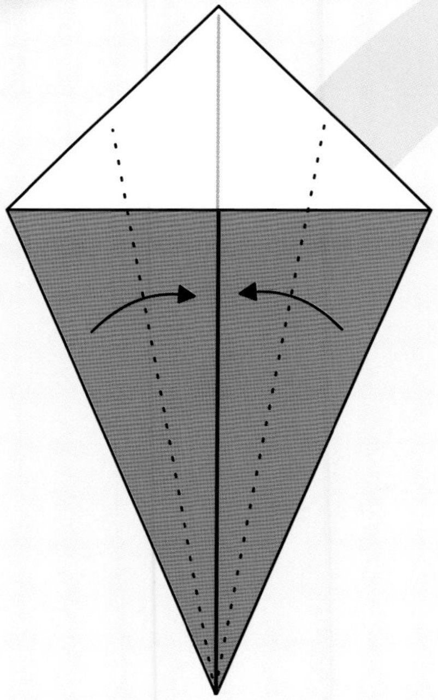

3

FOLD THE SIDES IN AGAIN TO
MEET THE CENTER LINE.

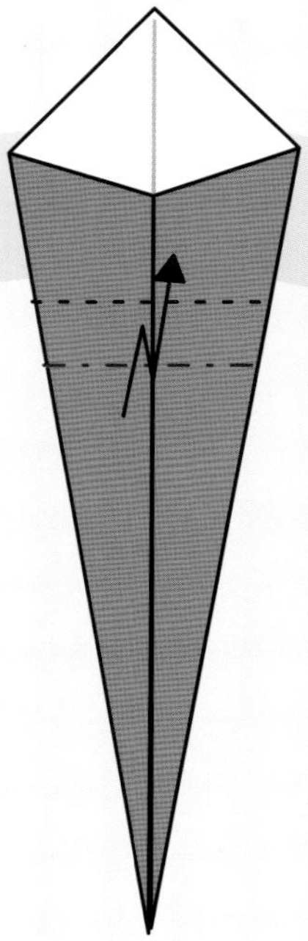

4

FIRST FOLD THE BOTTOM
CORNER TO THE BACK SIDE AS
SHOWN, THEN FOLD UP AGAIN
TO CREATE ONE ZIGZAG FOLD.
FLIP THE PIECE OVER.

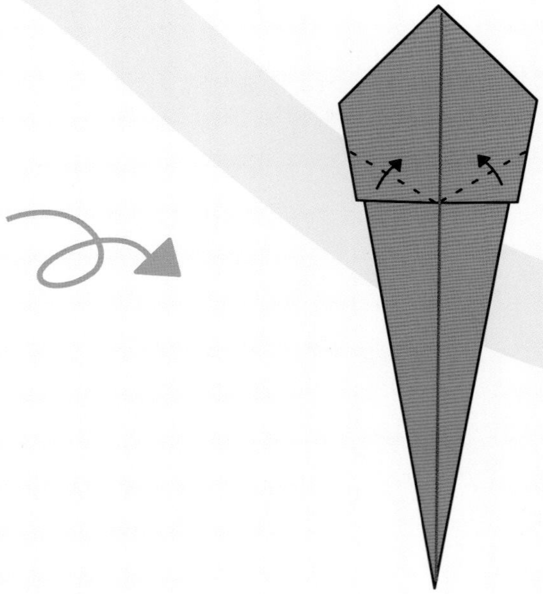

5

FOLD THE TWO SIDE
CORNERS UP.

6

FOLD THE ENTIRE PIECE
IN HALF TO CREATE THE
DEPTH OF THE SPOON.

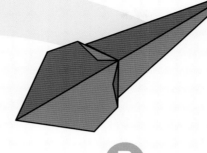

7

NOW YOU CAN EAT
SOME ICE CREAM WITH
YOUR SPOON!

nuinui

VIDEO: www.nuinui.ch/it/libro/origamoni-il-piccolo-chef/video/797

12 pot and lid

With the discovery of **fire**, prehistoric humans had the idea of roasting their meat before eating it. All you had to do was put the meat on a skewer and bring it close to the fire. But how do we cook other foods, such as grains? Simple: with a **container on or near the flame**. Early humans also began to use the shells of turtles or large mollusks as cooking pots and pans. When they learned to **heat clay to make it harden**, the first pots in terracotta were invented. Today pots and pans are made of **many different materials**, including various metals such as copper, aluminum, iron, stainless steel, and titanium, as well as glass, ceramic, stone, and clay.

DIFFICULTY 3

pot

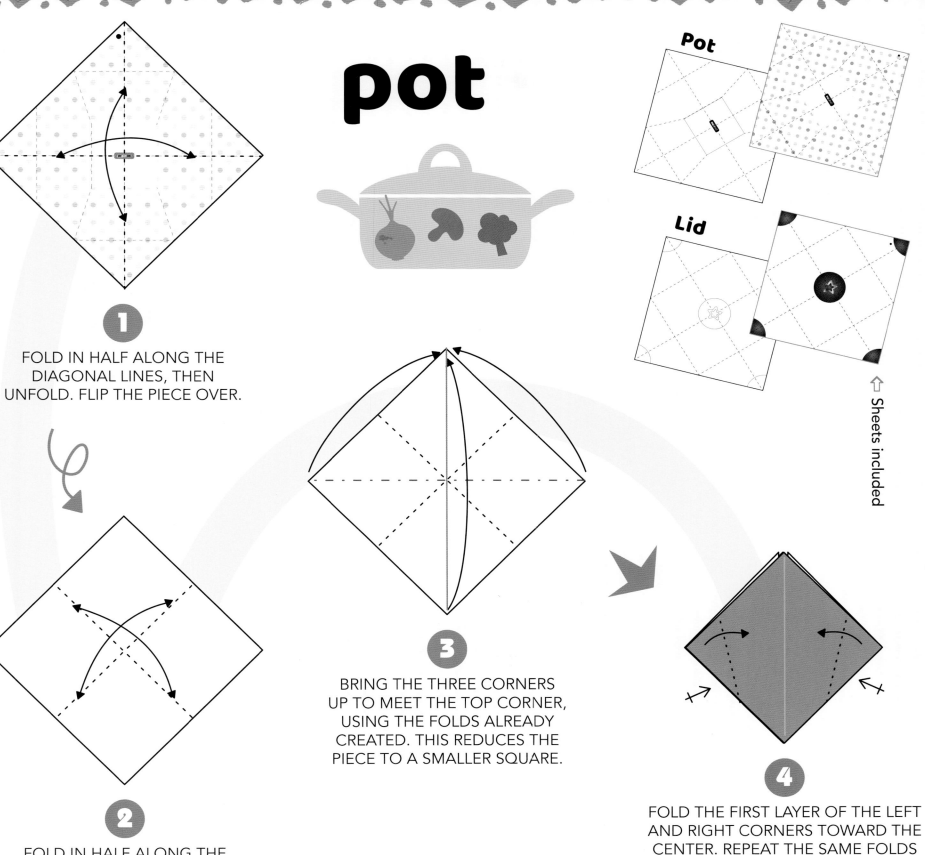

1

FOLD IN HALF ALONG THE DIAGONAL LINES, THEN UNFOLD. FLIP THE PIECE OVER.

2

FOLD IN HALF ALONG THE CENTER LINES, THEN UNFOLD.

3

BRING THE THREE CORNERS UP TO MEET THE TOP CORNER, USING THE FOLDS ALREADY CREATED. THIS REDUCES THE PIECE TO A SMALLER SQUARE.

4

FOLD THE FIRST LAYER OF THE LEFT AND RIGHT CORNERS TOWARD THE CENTER. REPEAT THE SAME FOLDS ON THE BACK OF THE PIECE.

Pot

Lid

⇧ Sheets included

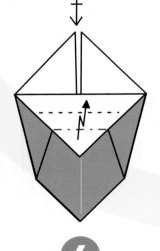

5

FOLD THE FIRST LAYER OF THE TOP CORNER DOWN. REPEAT THE SAME FOLD ON THE BACK OF THE PIECE.

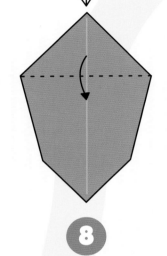

8

FOLD THE TOP CORNER DOWN. REPEAT THE SAME FOLD ON THE BACK OF THE PIECE.

6

FOLD A ZIGZAG ON THE FRONT OF THE PIECE WITH TWO FOLDS, FIRST UP AND THEN DOWN. REPEAT THE SAME FOLDS ON THE BACK OF THE PIECE.

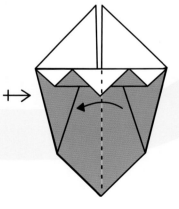

7

FOLD THE RIGHT SIDE TO THE LEFT. REPEAT THE SAME FOLD ON THE BACK OF THE PIECE.

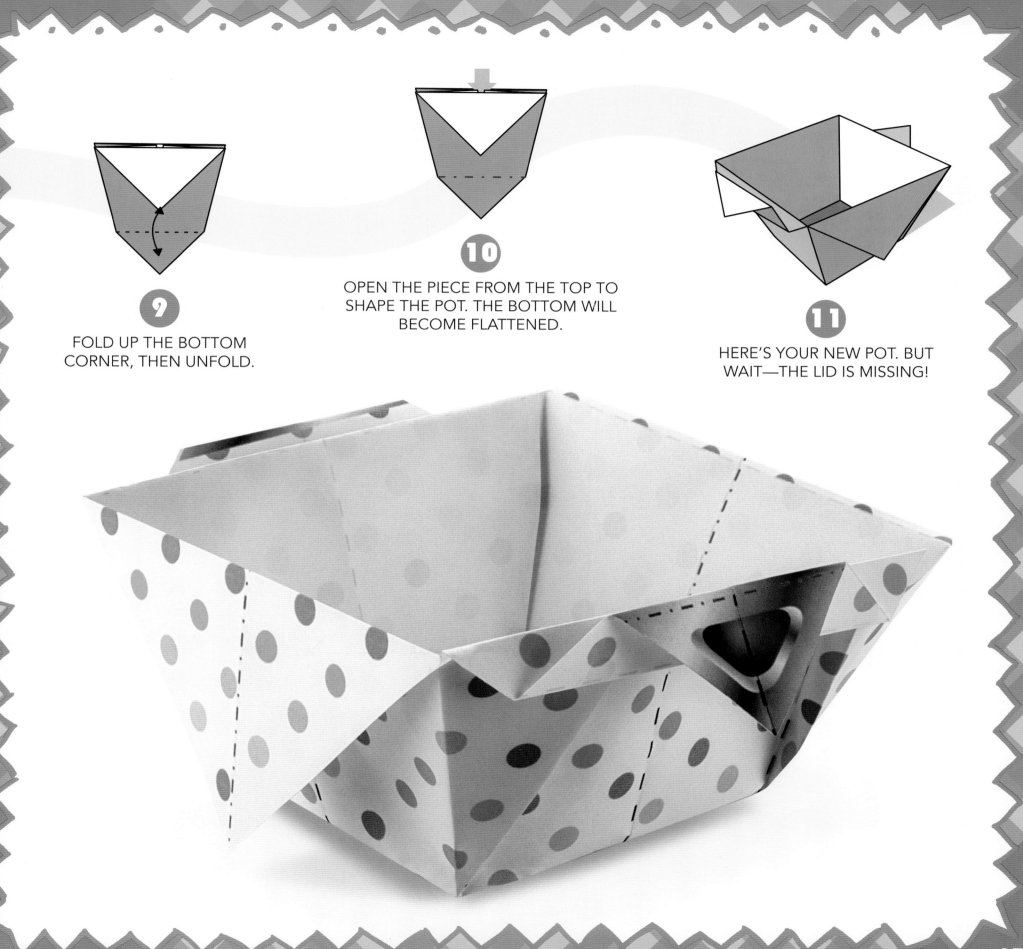

9

FOLD UP THE BOTTOM CORNER, THEN UNFOLD.

10

OPEN THE PIECE FROM THE TOP TO SHAPE THE POT. THE BOTTOM WILL BECOME FLATTENED.

11

HERE'S YOUR NEW POT. BUT WAIT—THE LID IS MISSING!

lid

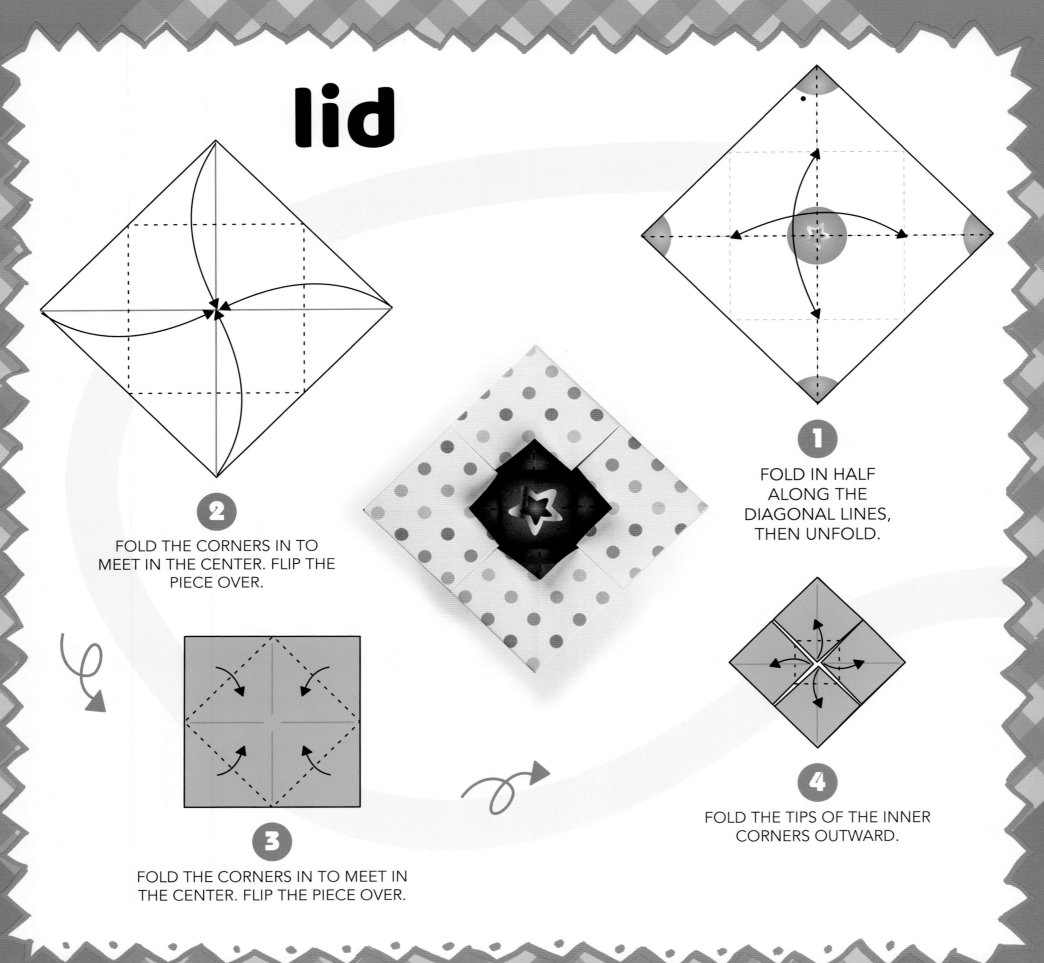

1 FOLD IN HALF ALONG THE DIAGONAL LINES, THEN UNFOLD.

2 FOLD THE CORNERS IN TO MEET IN THE CENTER. FLIP THE PIECE OVER.

3 FOLD THE CORNERS IN TO MEET IN THE CENTER. FLIP THE PIECE OVER.

4 FOLD THE TIPS OF THE INNER CORNERS OUTWARD.

5

NOW YOU CAN
COVER YOUR POT!

VIDEO: www.nuinui.ch/it/libro/origamoni-il-piccolo-chef/video/798

13 orange

Here is a **tasty fruit** that can be consumed raw after removing only the skin! But it can also be transformed into a **sweet, delicious juice**. Oranges are a citrus fruit that grow on large trees. There are many other varieties of this citrus, including **mandarin oranges** and **tangerines**. Oranges contain a lot of **vitamin C**, which helps to prevent the flu and colds.

⇧ Sheets included

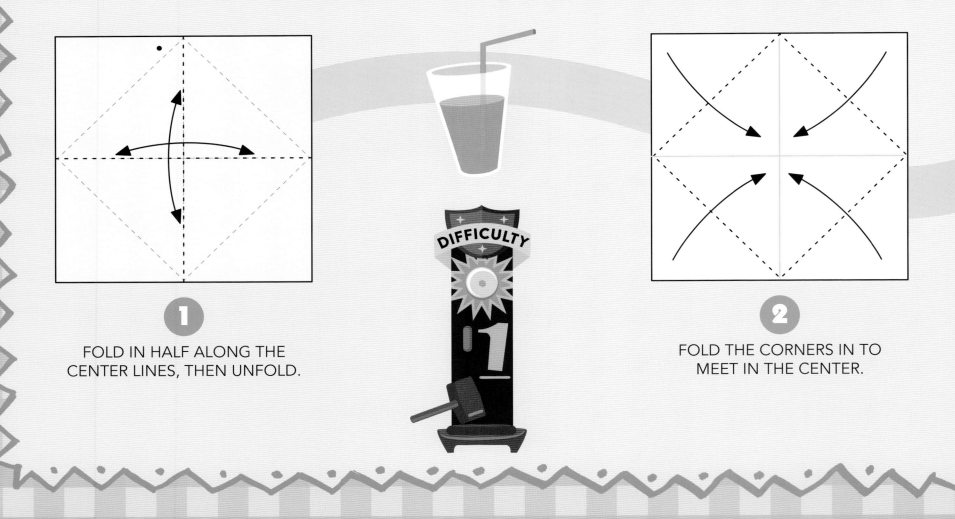

1

FOLD IN HALF ALONG THE CENTER LINES, THEN UNFOLD.

DIFFICULTY

1

2

FOLD THE CORNERS IN TO MEET IN THE CENTER.

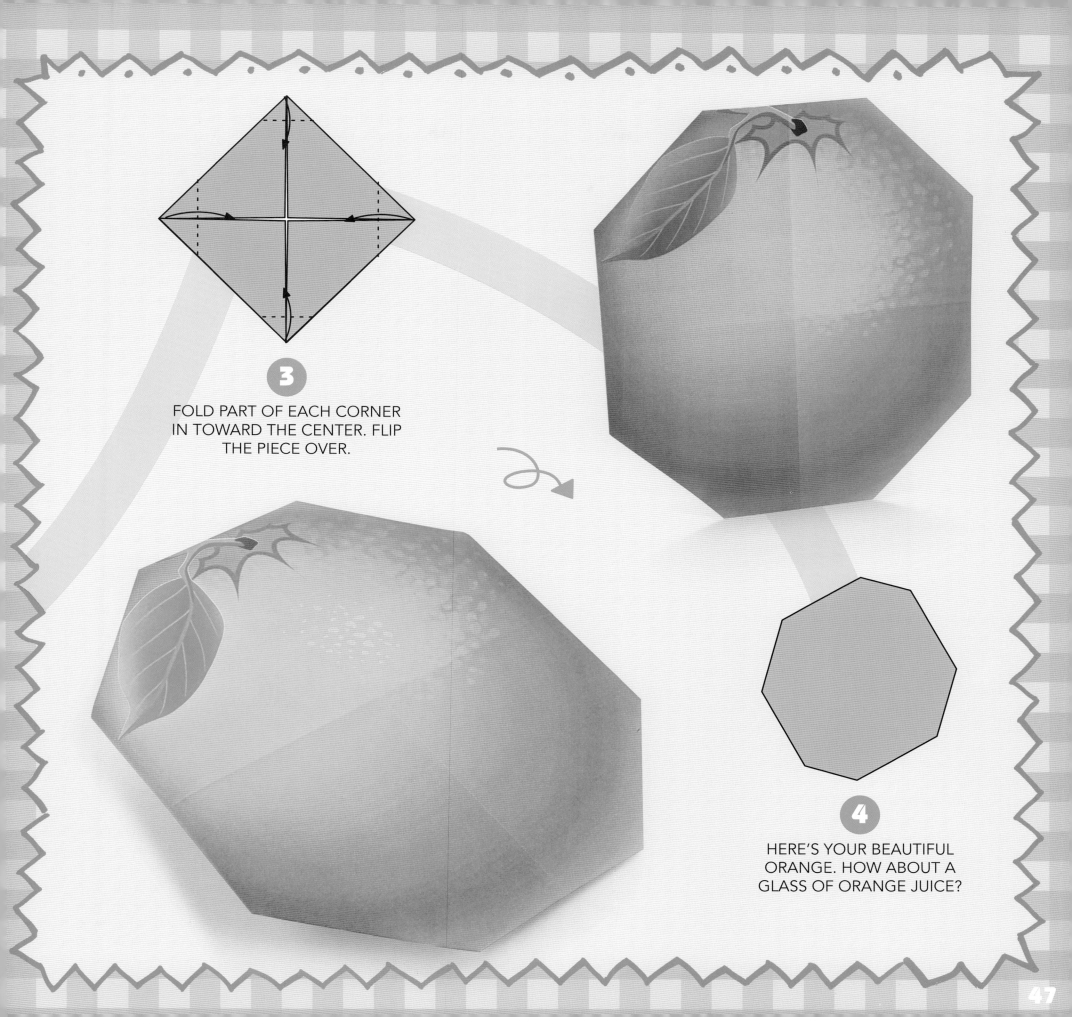

3

FOLD PART OF EACH CORNER IN TOWARD THE CENTER. FLIP THE PIECE OVER.

4

HERE'S YOUR BEAUTIFUL ORANGE. HOW ABOUT A GLASS OF ORANGE JUICE?

VIDEO: www.nuinui.ch/it/libro/origamoni-il-piccolo-chef/video/799

14 bowl

Containers of this type, made of clay, were used since very ancient times. Traces of bowls have been found in many **prehistoric sites** all over the world. A broken bowl discovered in an archeology excavation can tell us much of the history of the people who used the bowl and can even tell us which foods fed a certain group of people. Even today these ancient items are essential in the kitchen and are **made of many different materials**: wood, glass, plastic, porcelain, stainless steel, and more. Each type of bowl has a specific use. It is hard to imagine a kitchen that does not include bowls in its cabinets!

⇧ Sheets included

⇦ Includes extra coloring origami sheet so you can make a set of bowls!

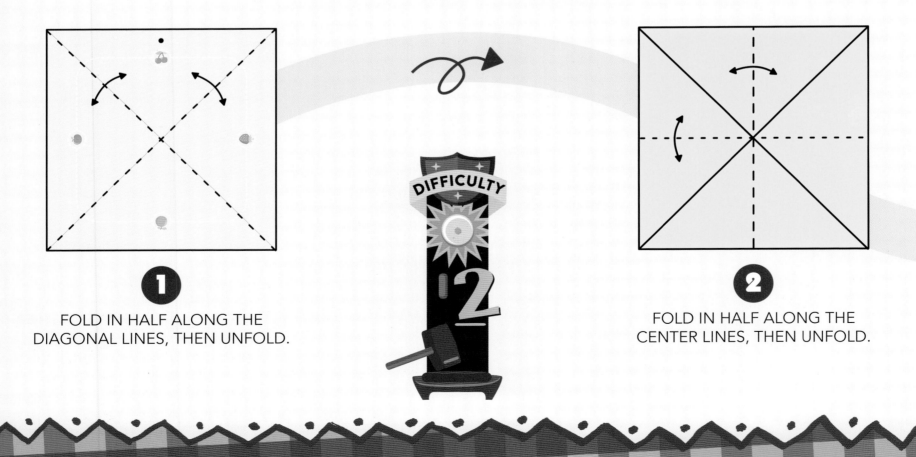

1 FOLD IN HALF ALONG THE DIAGONAL LINES, THEN UNFOLD.

DIFFICULTY 2

2 FOLD IN HALF ALONG THE CENTER LINES, THEN UNFOLD.

48

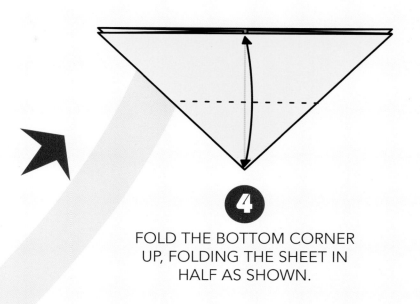

4

FOLD THE BOTTOM CORNER UP, FOLDING THE SHEET IN HALF AS SHOWN.

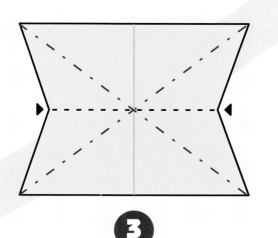

3

USING THE FOLDS ALREADY MADE, FOLD THE PAPER IN HALF TO THE BACK SIDE AS SHOWN WHILE PUSHING UP THE SIDE FOLDS, CREATING A TRIANGLE WITH FOUR FLAPS. BE CAREFUL: THE CENTER OF THE SHEET MUST FOLD UP TOWARD YOU!

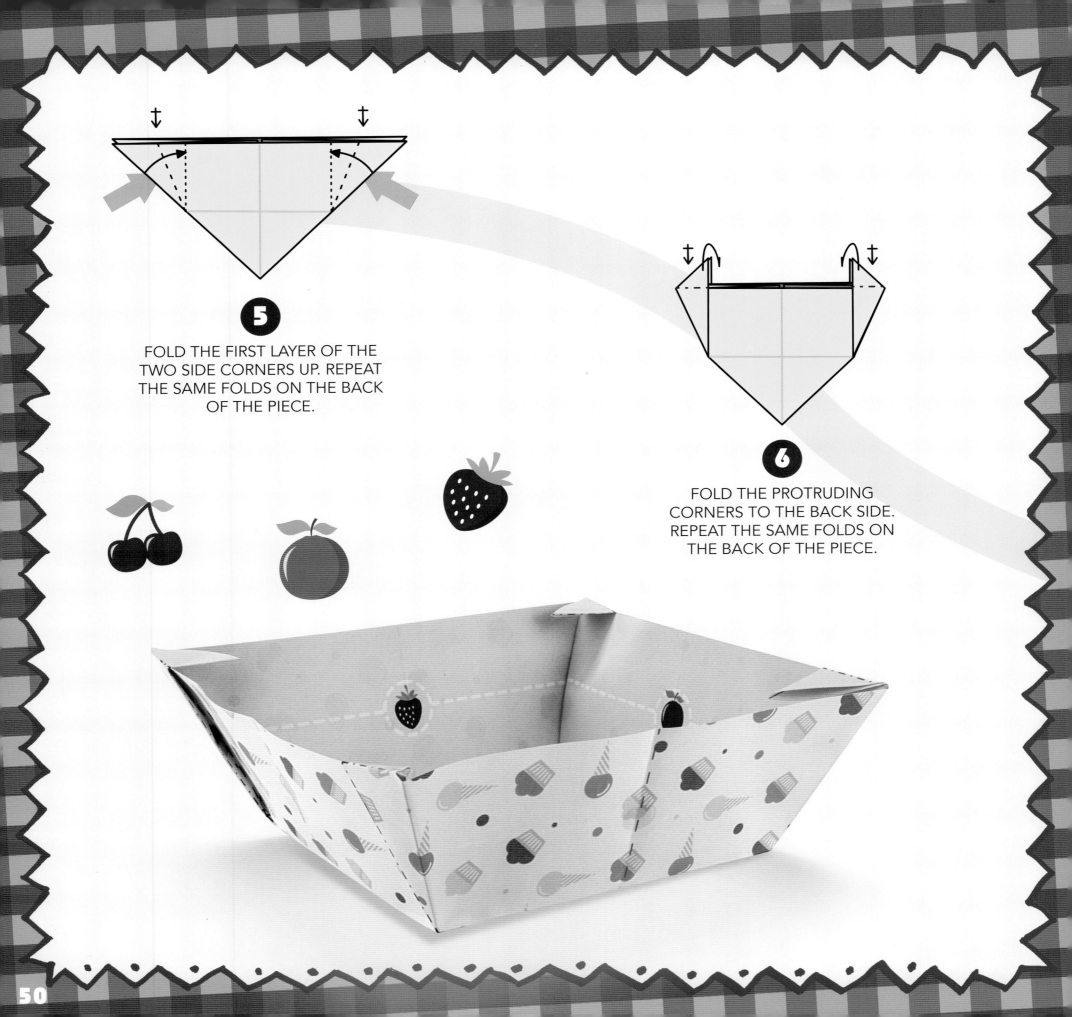

5

FOLD THE FIRST LAYER OF THE TWO SIDE CORNERS UP. REPEAT THE SAME FOLDS ON THE BACK OF THE PIECE.

6

FOLD THE PROTRUDING CORNERS TO THE BACK SIDE. REPEAT THE SAME FOLDS ON THE BACK OF THE PIECE.

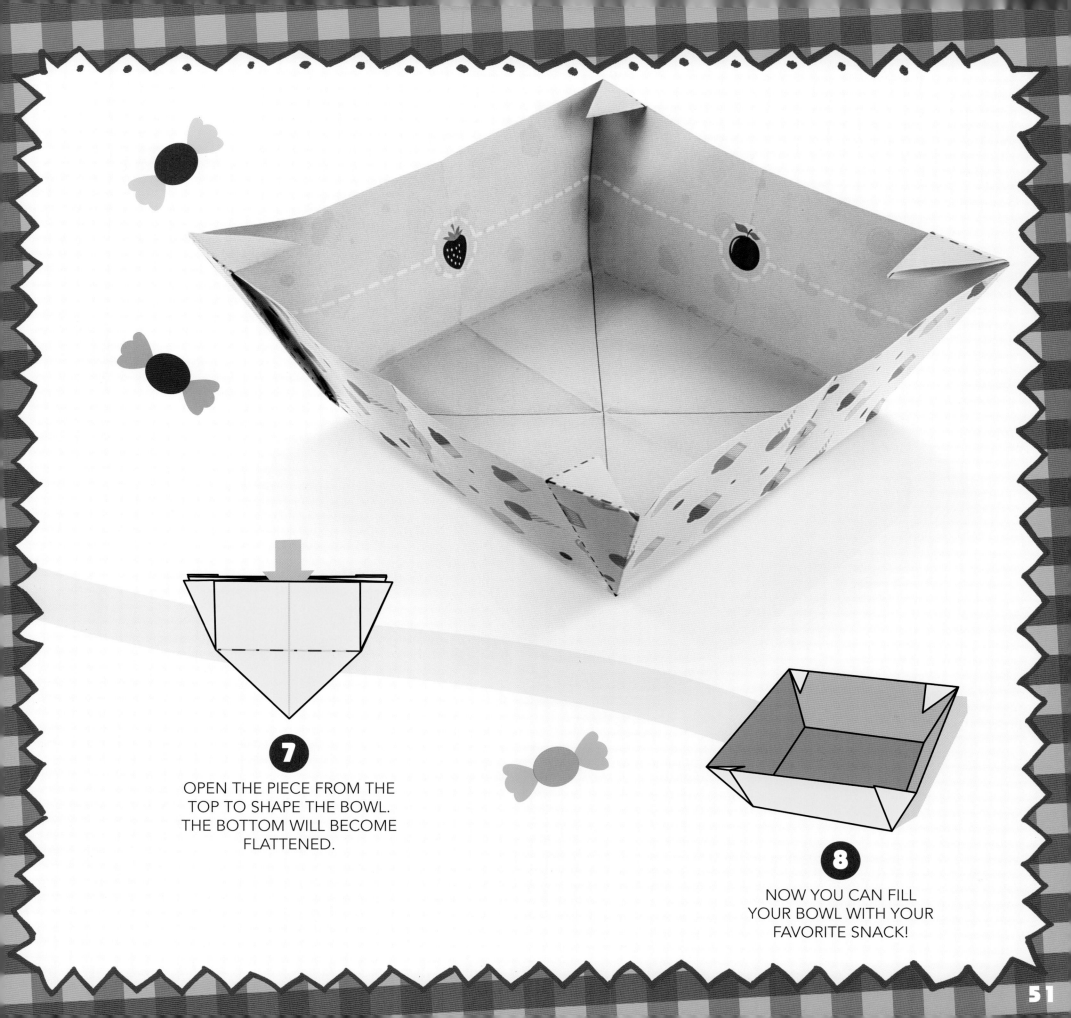

7

OPEN THE PIECE FROM THE TOP TO SHAPE THE BOWL. THE BOTTOM WILL BECOME FLATTENED.

8

NOW YOU CAN FILL YOUR BOWL WITH YOUR FAVORITE SNACK!

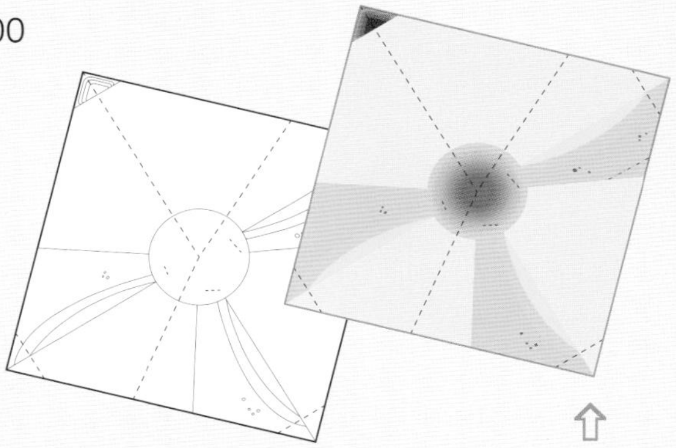

⇧ Sheets included

15 bananas

Bananas are a **fruit** that can be used in many different ways—to prepare cakes, desserts, biscuits, or drinks, all delicious foods that are very rich in nutrients important for our health. The word "banana" came from **Africa** to the west through Portuguese and Spanish. It then became part of other languages.

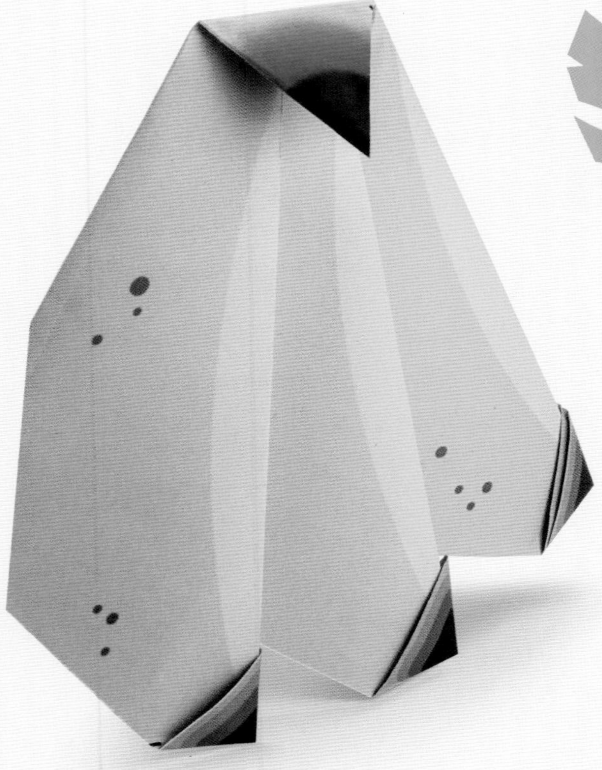

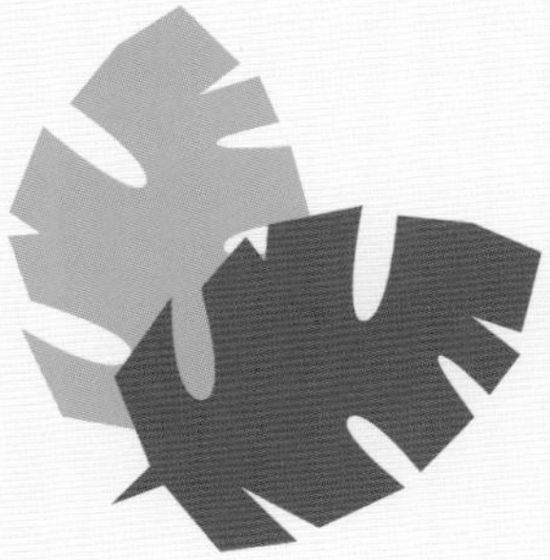

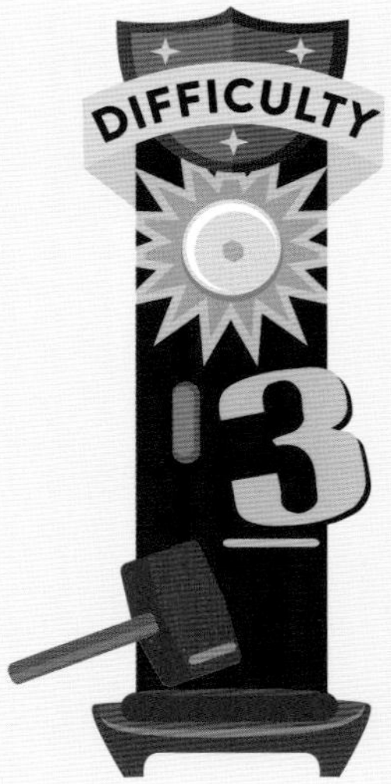

DIFFICULTY

3

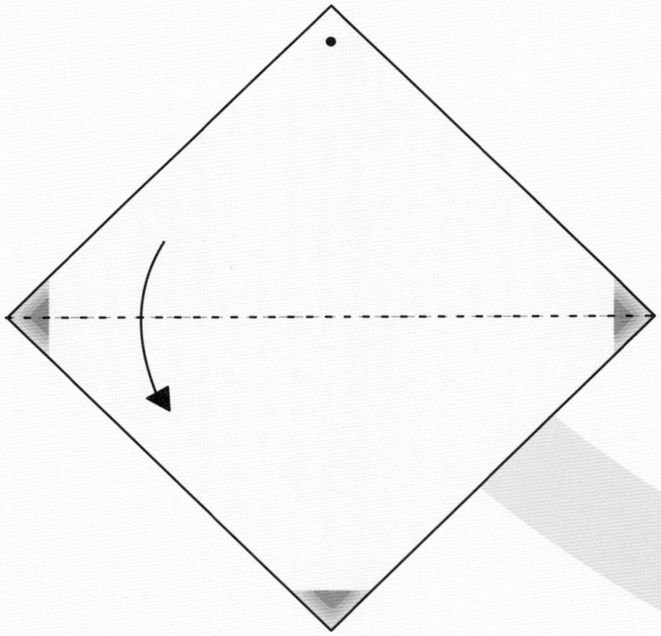

1

FOLD IN HALF ALONG THE HORIZONTAL DIAGONAL LINE.

3

FOLD THE FIRST LAYER ONLY
DOWN AS SHOWN.

2

FOLD IN HALF AGAIN TO
THE LEFT.

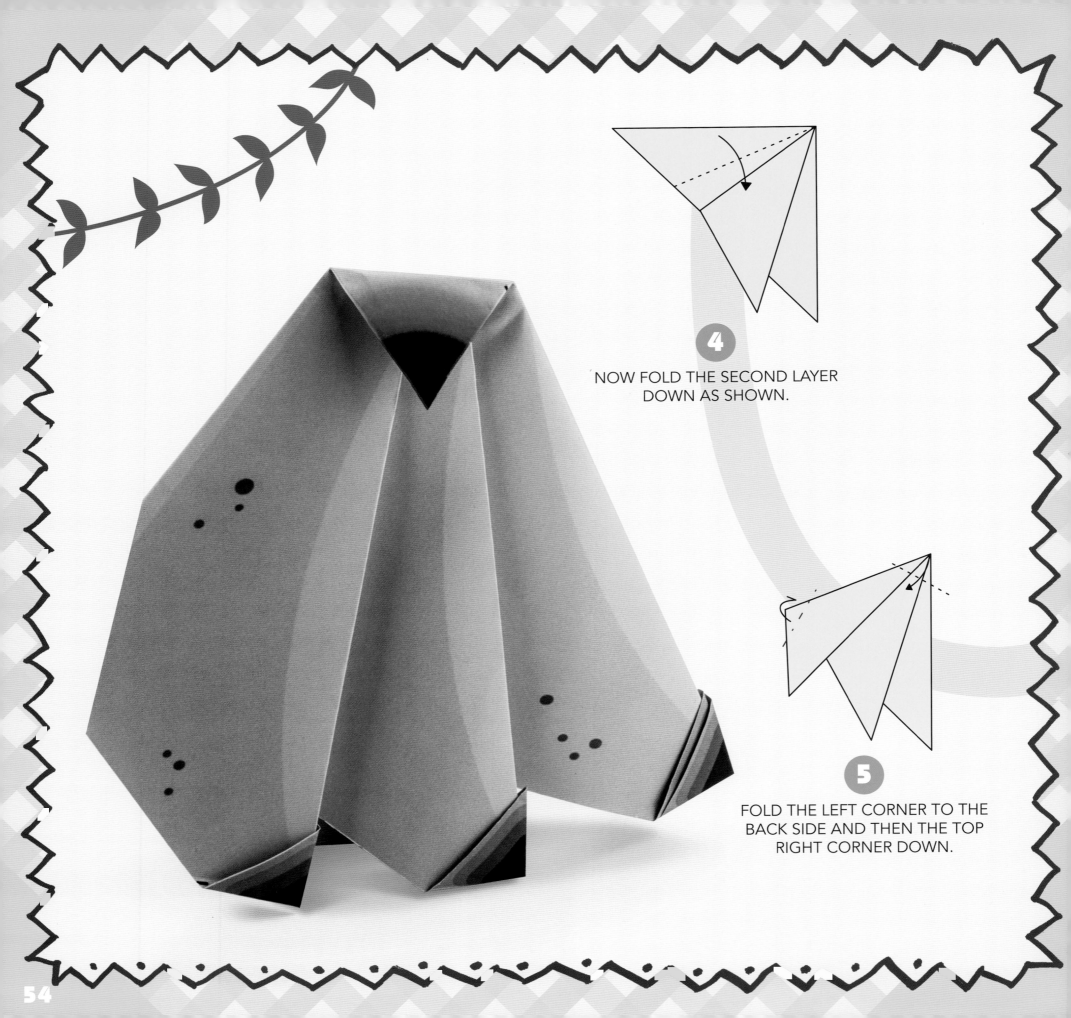

4

NOW FOLD THE SECOND LAYER DOWN AS SHOWN.

5

FOLD THE LEFT CORNER TO THE BACK SIDE AND THEN THE TOP RIGHT CORNER DOWN.

6

FOLD UP THE CORNER OF EACH
OF THE THREE BANANAS.

7

YOUR BANANAS ARE RIPE AND
READY TO GO!

VIDEO: www.nuinui.ch/it/libro/origamoni-il-piccolo-chef/video/801

⇧ Sheets included

16 apple

Apples grow on trees that also grow magnificent **apple blossoms** and are very popular everywhere. Apples have an important place in **stories such as Snow White** where the young princess is tricked by the evil queen who offers her a poison apple. This fruit can be eaten just as it is, **without even peeling** it, but remember to wash it very well before you bite into it. You can also make pie from apples—it's delicious!

1

FOLD IN HALF ALONG THE HORIZONTAL CENTER LINE.

DIFFICULTY **2**

2

FOLD IN HALF AGAIN, THEN UNFOLD.

3

FOLD THE SIDES IN TO MEET THE
CENTER LINE, THEN UNFOLD.

4

FOLD THE SIDES IN TO
MEET THE FOLD LINES
YOU JUST CREATED.

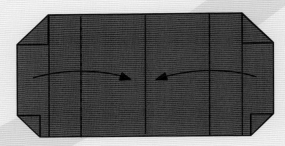

6

FOLD THE SIDES IN TO MEET
THE CENTER LINE.

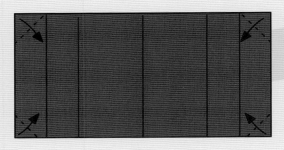

5

FOLD THE TIPS OF THE FOUR
CORNERS INWARD.

7

FOLD THE FOUR CORNERS TO THE BACK SIDE.

8

HERE IS YOUR FRESH APPLE. DOESN'T IT SMELL GREAT?

⇧ Sheets included

17 knife

This tool has existed since **ancient times**. The first knives were crafted by prehistoric people with pieces of **stone chipped to produce a sharpened edge** with which to cut, scrape, and chop food. Later, when humans learned to work with iron and bronze, the first metal knives were invented. In today's kitchens, different **types of knives** are used according to the food to be cut. Since they are sharp tools that can make it easy to cut yourself, knives need to be handled with **extreme care**.

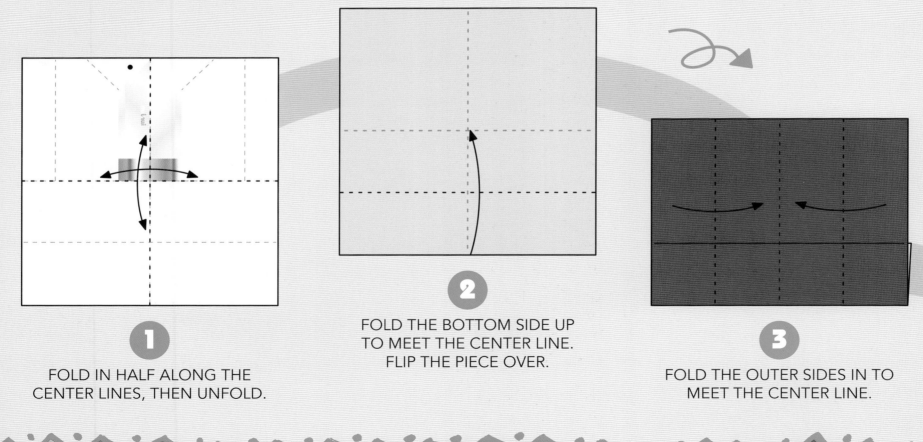

1
FOLD IN HALF ALONG THE CENTER LINES, THEN UNFOLD.

2
FOLD THE BOTTOM SIDE UP TO MEET THE CENTER LINE. FLIP THE PIECE OVER.

3
FOLD THE OUTER SIDES IN TO MEET THE CENTER LINE.

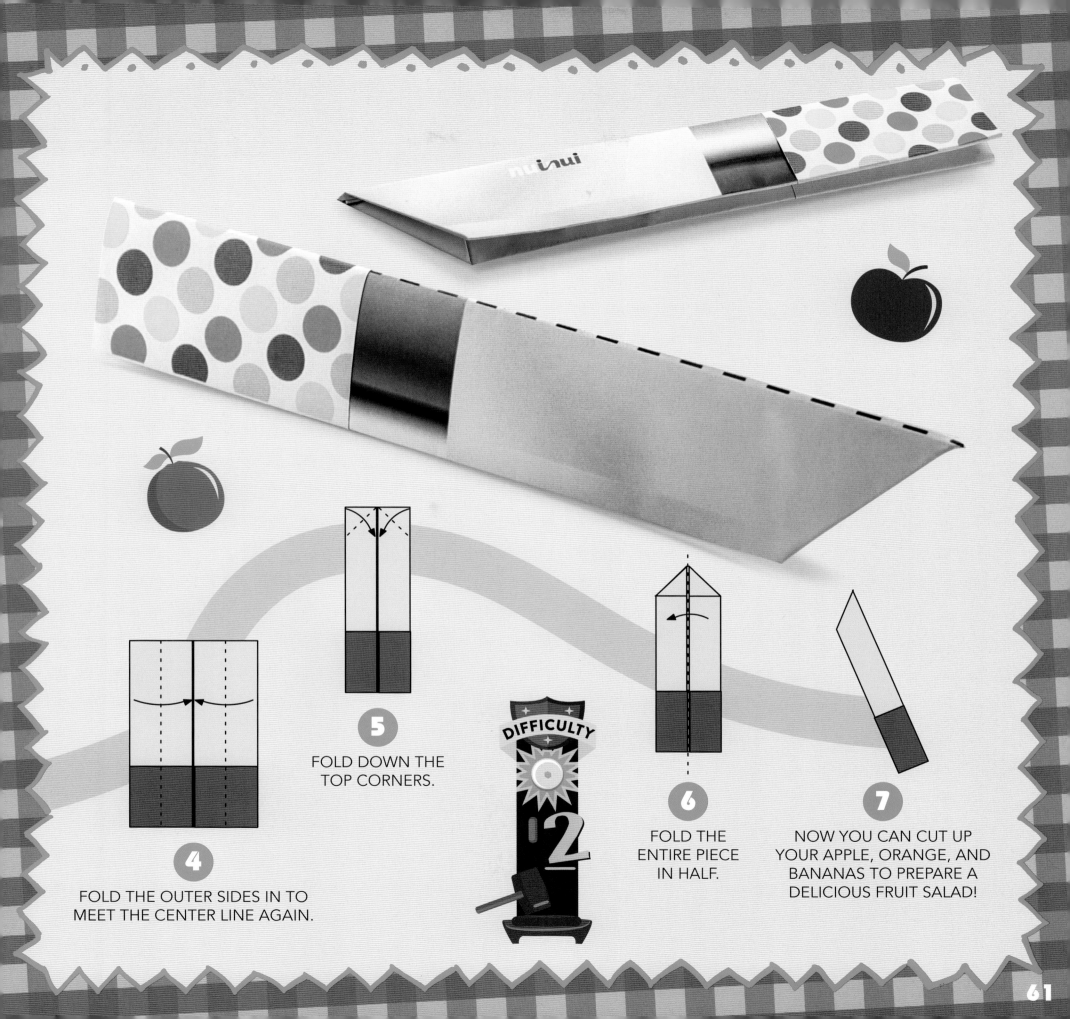

4 FOLD THE OUTER SIDES IN TO MEET THE CENTER LINE AGAIN.

5 FOLD DOWN THE TOP CORNERS.

DIFFICULTY 2

6 FOLD THE ENTIRE PIECE IN HALF.

7 NOW YOU CAN CUT UP YOUR APPLE, ORANGE, AND BANANAS TO PREPARE A DELICIOUS FRUIT SALAD!

nuinui

VIDEO: www.nuinui.ch/it/libro/origamoni-il-piccolo-chef/video/804

⇧ Sheets included

18 watermelon

Beautiful, juicy, and very **rich in water**, watermelons have a hard green skin and a **tasty red pulp**. They grow from huge climbing vines. You'll often find large black seeds or small white seeds in your watermelon slices—they're all safe to eat! You can also prepare **watermelon juice**. My little secret is to add a few mint leaves to the juice for extra flavor.

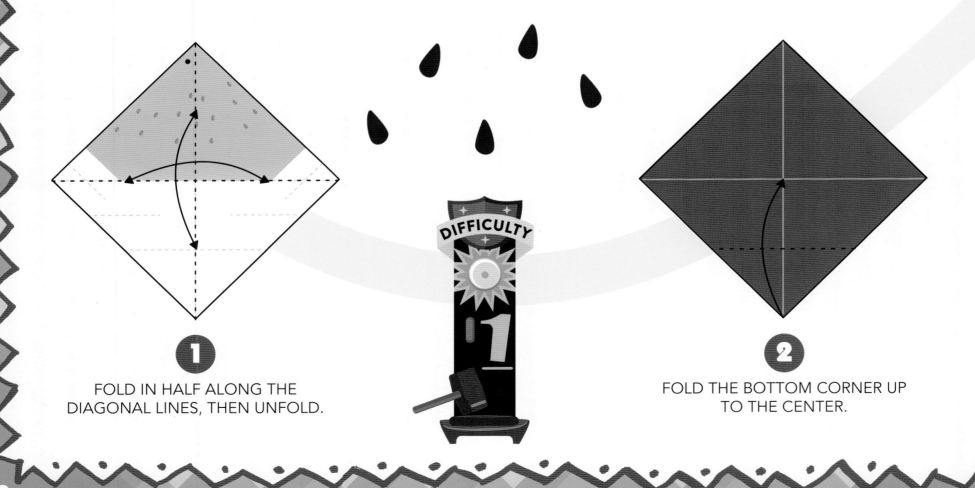

1

FOLD IN HALF ALONG THE
DIAGONAL LINES, THEN UNFOLD.

DIFFICULTY
1

2

FOLD THE BOTTOM CORNER UP
TO THE CENTER.

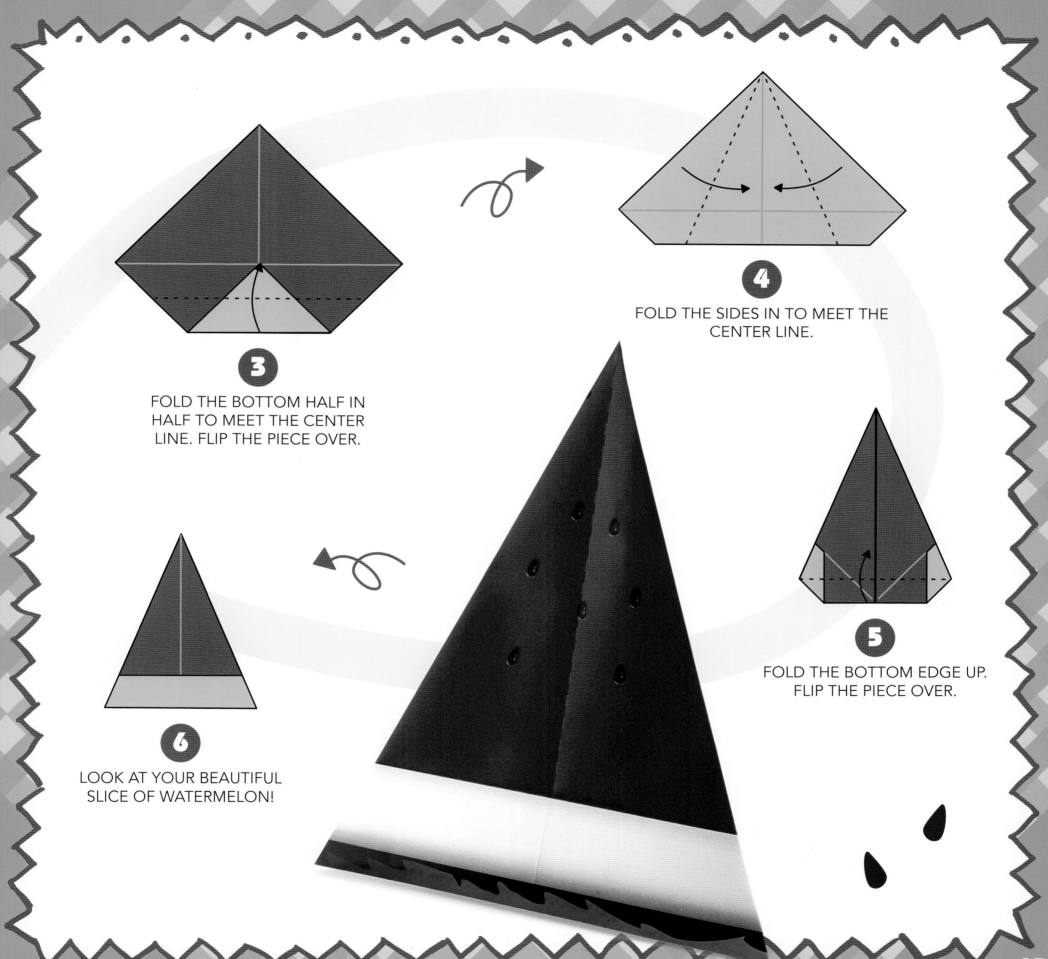

3

FOLD THE BOTTOM HALF IN HALF TO MEET THE CENTER LINE. FLIP THE PIECE OVER.

4

FOLD THE SIDES IN TO MEET THE CENTER LINE.

5

FOLD THE BOTTOM EDGE UP. FLIP THE PIECE OVER.

6

LOOK AT YOUR BEAUTIFUL SLICE OF WATERMELON!

⇧ Sheets included

19 cabbage

Cabbage, a very popular food since the **Middle Ages**, is a fundamental ingredient in cooking. It is prepared in many different ways, cooked or raw, and is very rich in fiber and vitamins K and C. Particularly well-known is **sauerkraut,** which is a classic dish typical in every German kitchen, made from **fermented cabbage**. The process of fermentation increases the nutritional value, especially B vitamins and healthy enzymes.

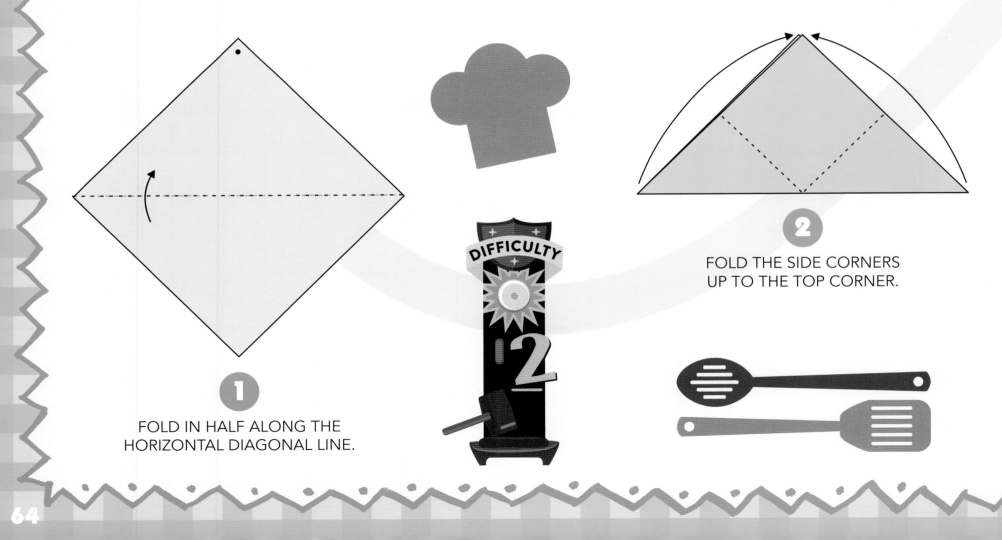

DIFFICULTY 2

1 FOLD IN HALF ALONG THE HORIZONTAL DIAGONAL LINE.

2 FOLD THE SIDE CORNERS UP TO THE TOP CORNER.

3

FOLD THE FIRST LAYER OF EACH OF THE INNER CORNERS TOWARD THE OUTSIDE.

4

FOLD THE TOP AND BOTTOM CORNERS TO THE BACK SIDE.

5

HERE IS YOUR HOMEGROWN CABBAGE, READY TO BE COOKED!

VIDEO: www.nuinui.ch/it/libro/origamoni-il-piccolo-chef/video/805

20 CUP

We use cups to **drink coffee, tea, and hot chocolate**, of course, but they are also an important part of cooking. When a cook creates a dish, they generally proceed in a very personal and almost intuitive way, but if they have to **explain how to make the recipe** to others who want to follow their recipe, they will need to communicate **accurate amounts of the ingredients** to use, such as flour, oil, or milk. Because of this, cups have become a well-known unit of measurement in the kitchen.

⇧ Sheets included
⇦ Includes extra coloring origami sheet so you can make a set of cups!

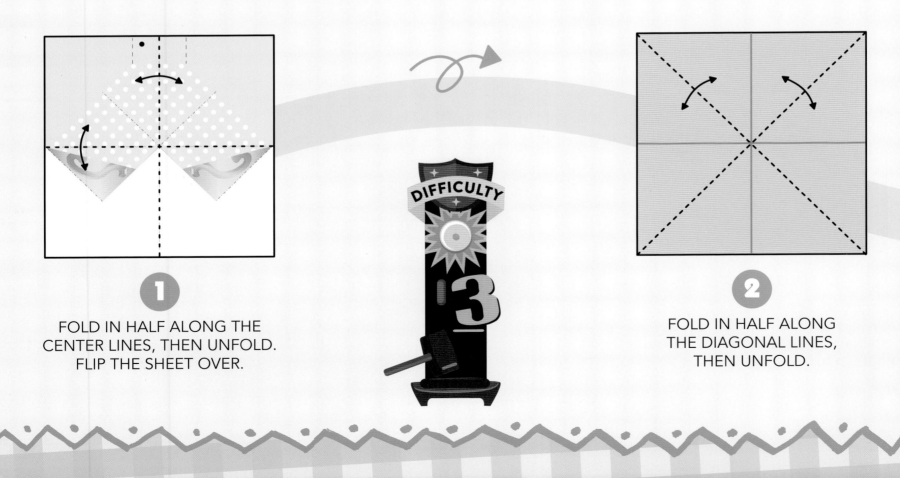

1
FOLD IN HALF ALONG THE CENTER LINES, THEN UNFOLD. FLIP THE SHEET OVER.

DIFFICULTY **3**

2
FOLD IN HALF ALONG THE DIAGONAL LINES, THEN UNFOLD.

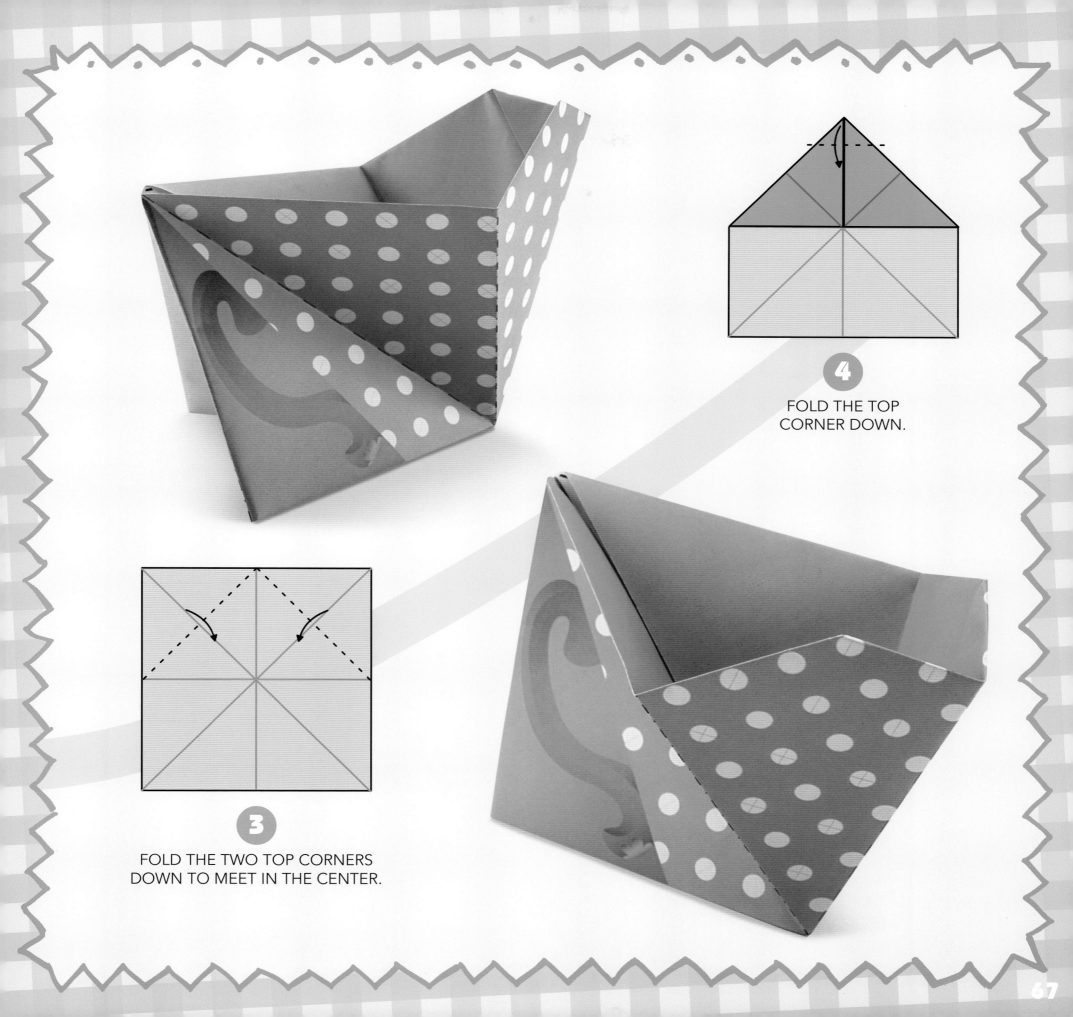

4

FOLD THE TOP
CORNER DOWN.

3

FOLD THE TWO TOP CORNERS
DOWN TO MEET IN THE CENTER.

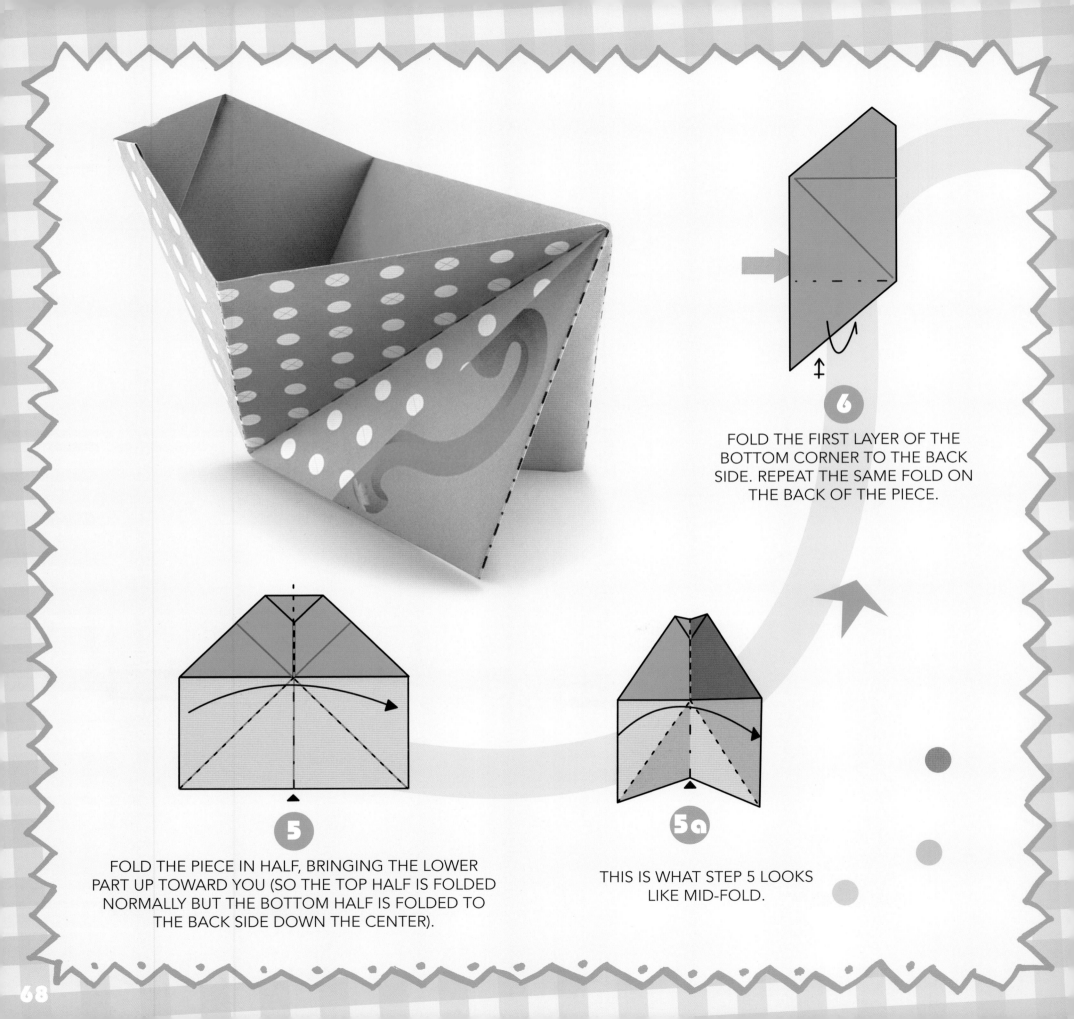

6

FOLD THE FIRST LAYER OF THE BOTTOM CORNER TO THE BACK SIDE. REPEAT THE SAME FOLD ON THE BACK OF THE PIECE.

5

FOLD THE PIECE IN HALF, BRINGING THE LOWER PART UP TOWARD YOU (SO THE TOP HALF IS FOLDED NORMALLY BUT THE BOTTOM HALF IS FOLDED TO THE BACK SIDE DOWN THE CENTER).

5a

THIS IS WHAT STEP 5 LOOKS LIKE MID-FOLD.

7

OPEN THE PIECE FROM THE SIDE TO SHAPE THE CUP.

8

NOW YOU CAN DRINK A DELICIOUS CUP OF YOUR FAVORITE BEVERAGE!

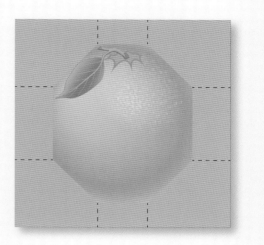

A simple sheet of paper transforms like magic . . .

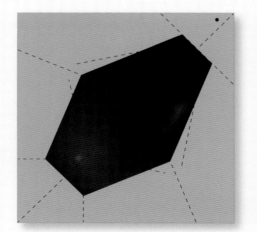

Rita Foelker, a writer and journalist with a master's degree in philosophy, is also, and above all, a mother. Born in Brazil, where she lives and works in the field of publishing as an author and illustrator, she has been studying and teaching the ancient Japanese art of origami since 1987 and has participated in various international projects. Her origami creations have been published in many countries, including in the journal of the prestigious British Origami Society. Author of numerous volumes of origami published in Brazil, she has created several books, including *Magic Origami*, *The Origami Garden*, *The Origami Galaxy*, *Relaxing Origami Mandalas*, and *Awesome Origami*. Visit her at her website: **http://rfoelker.wix.com/superorigami**

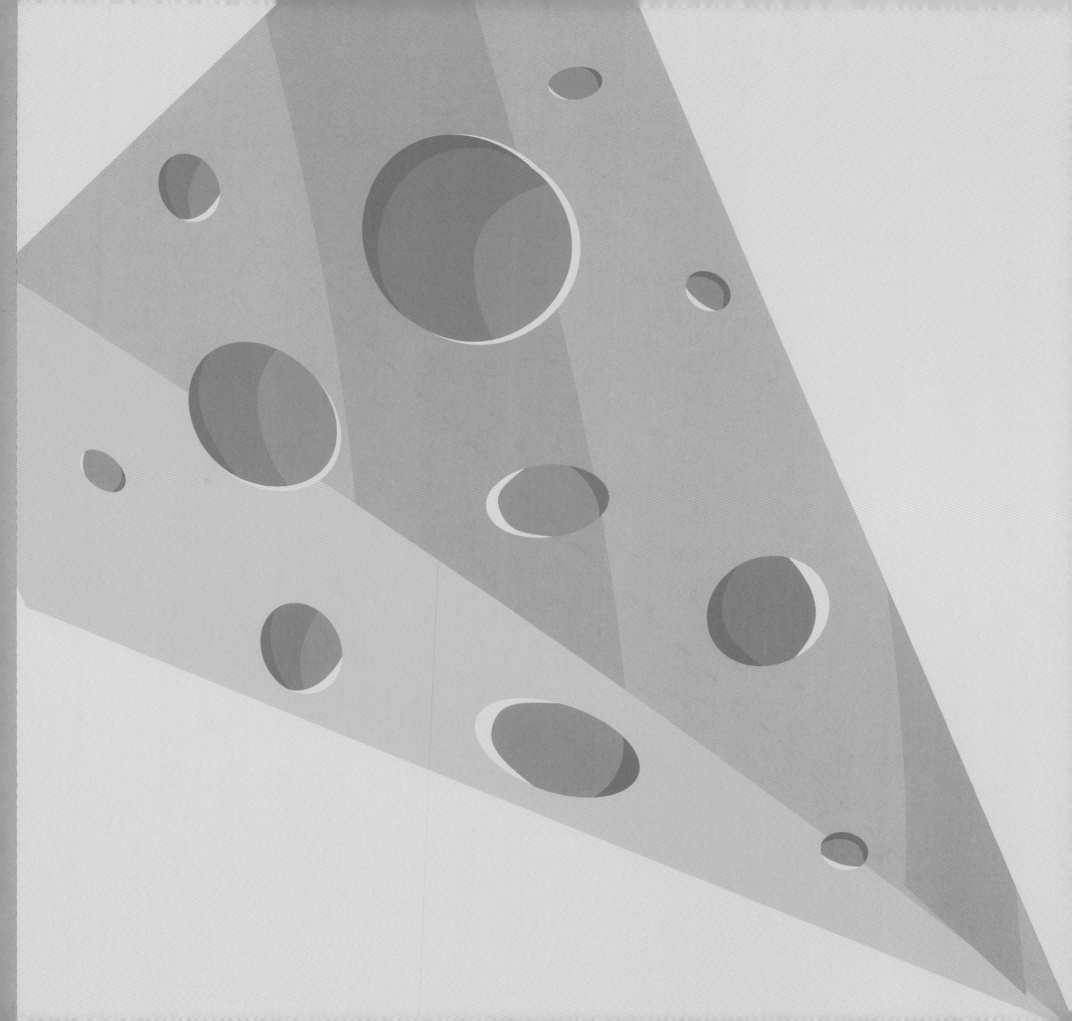

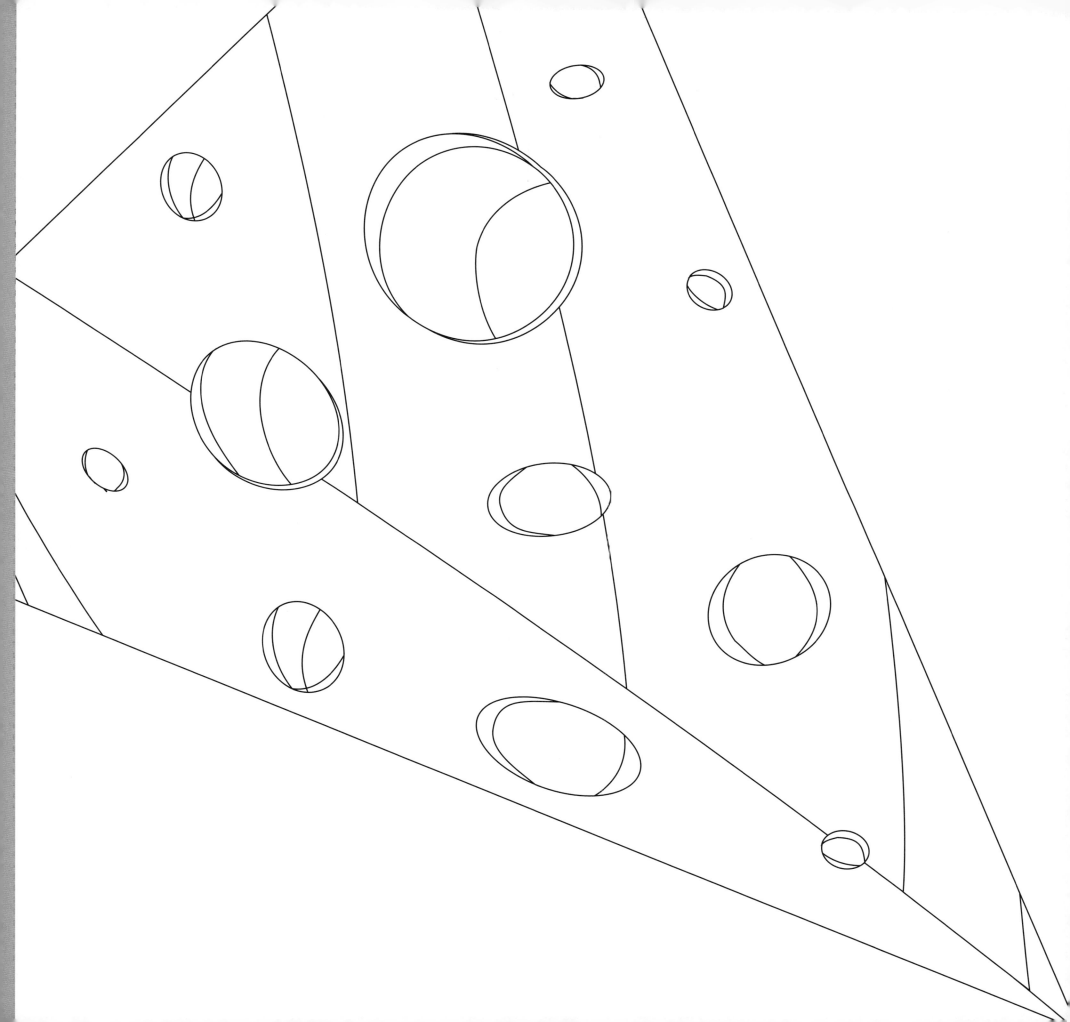

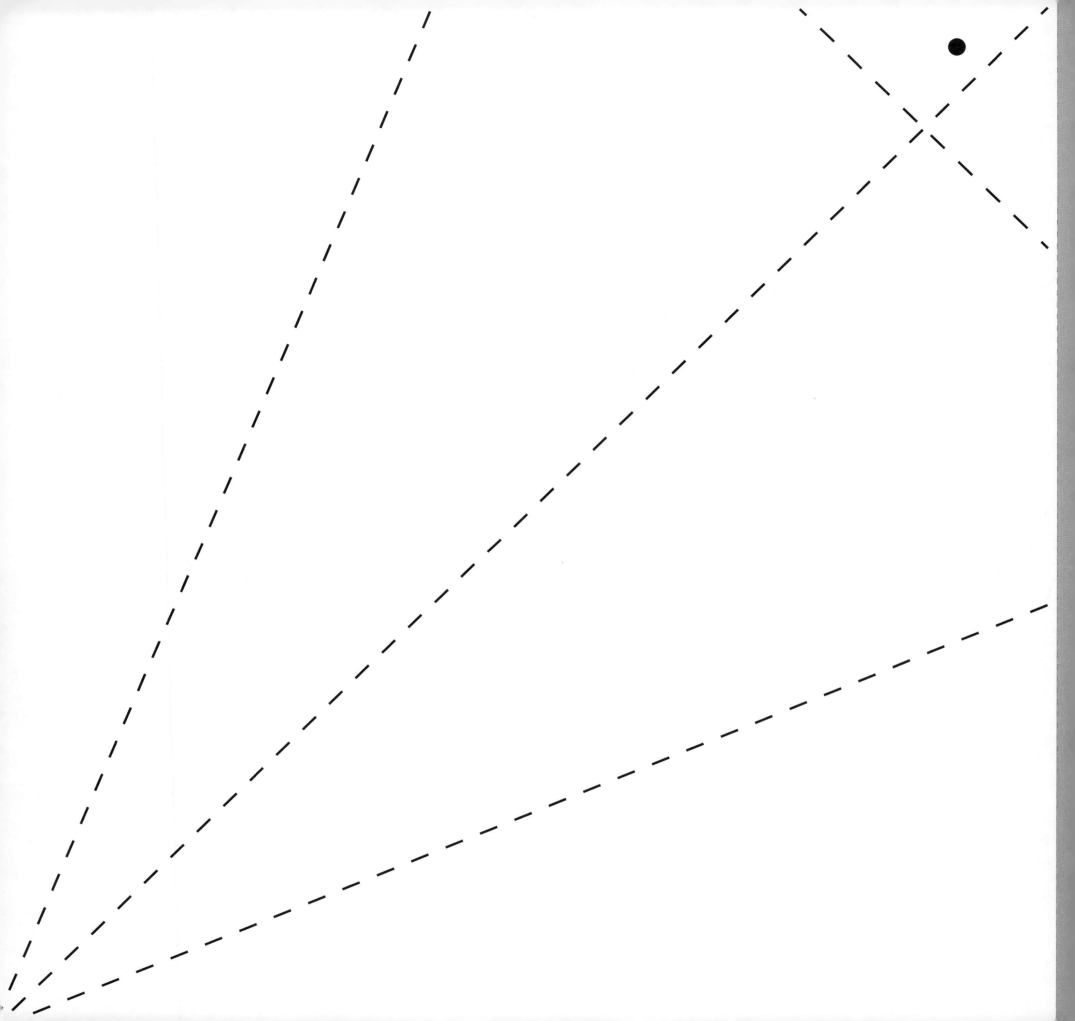

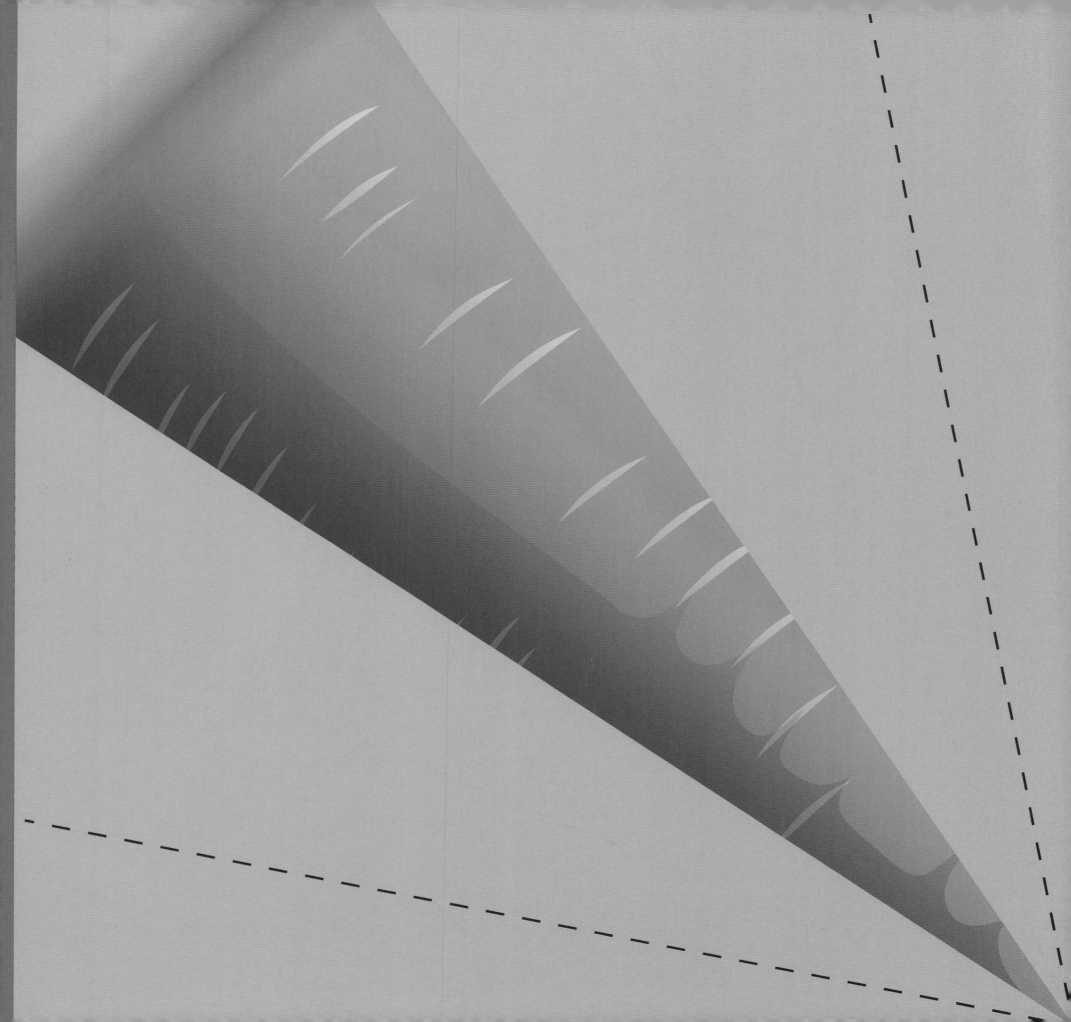

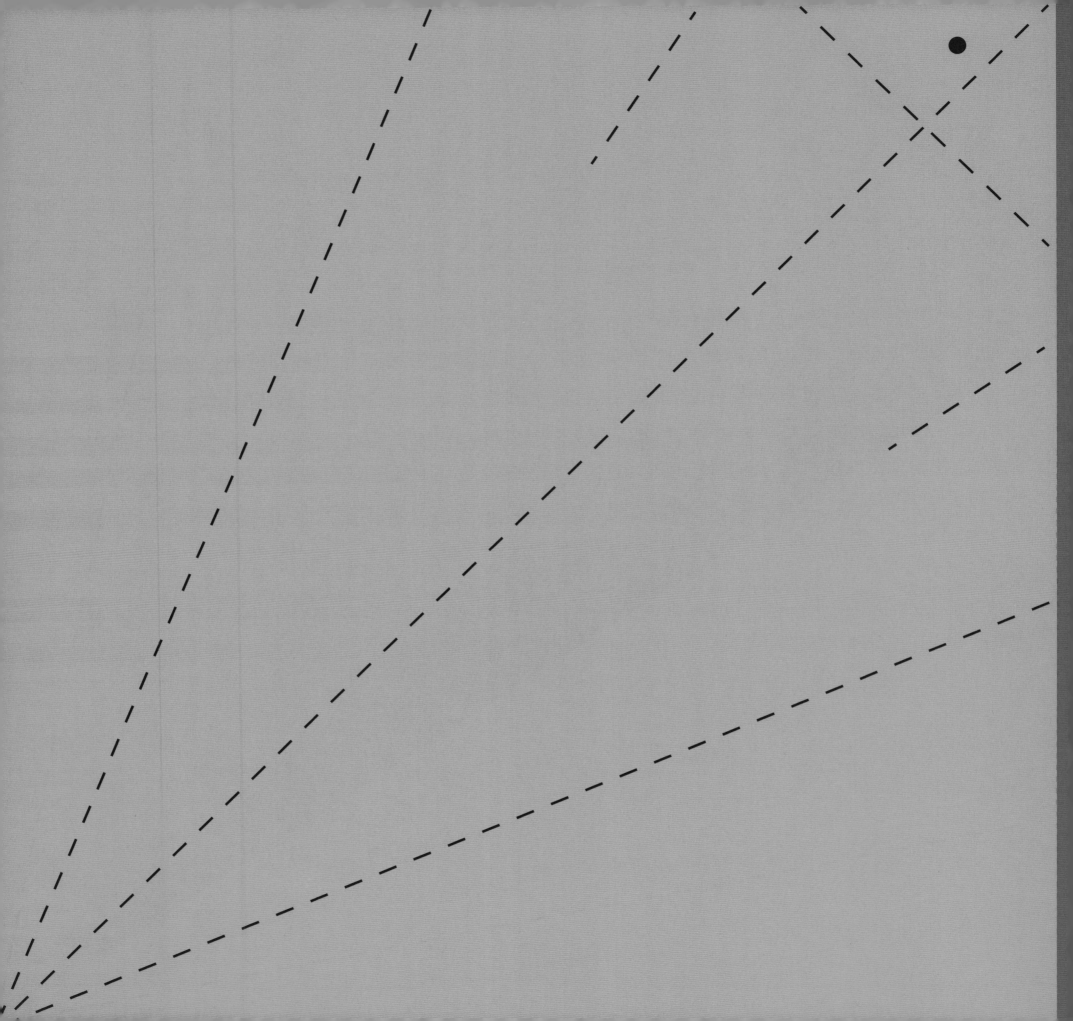

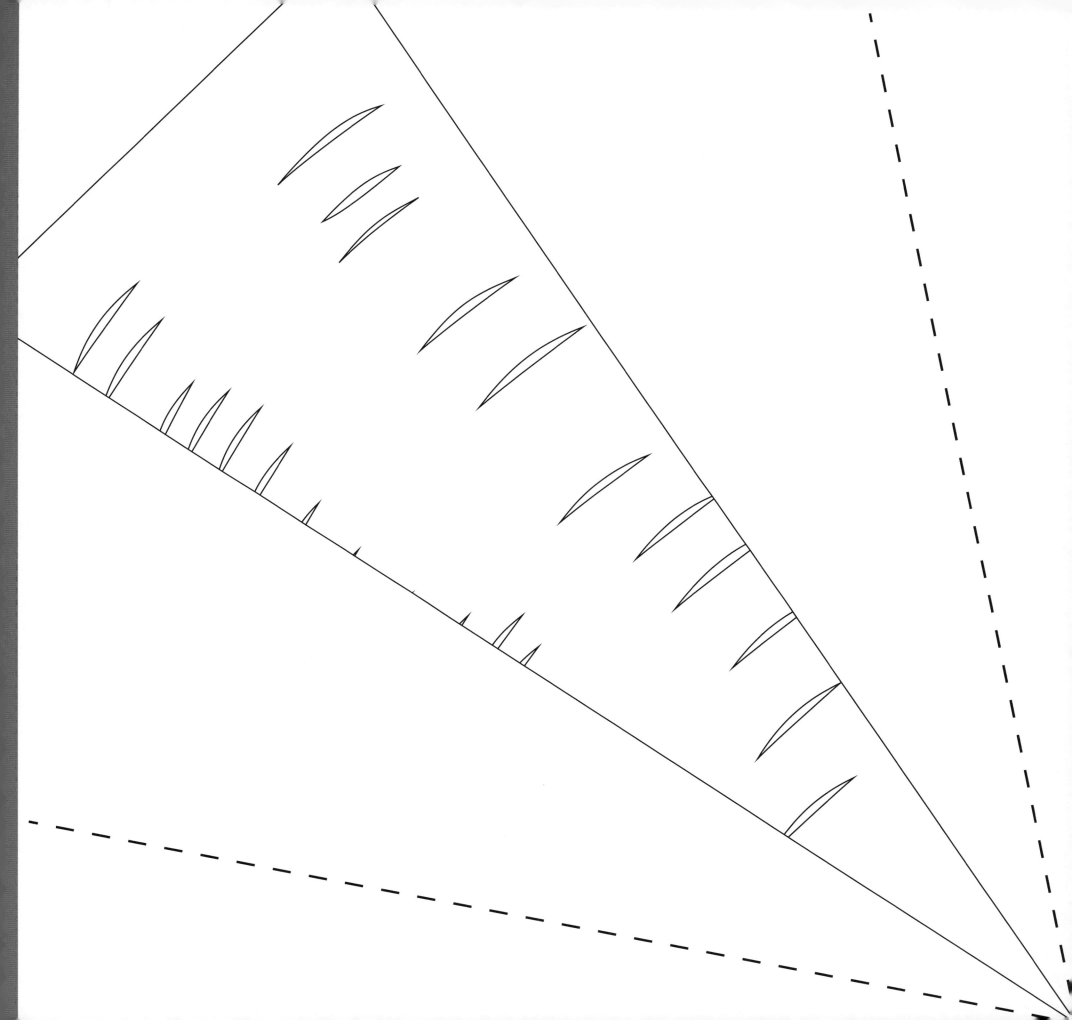

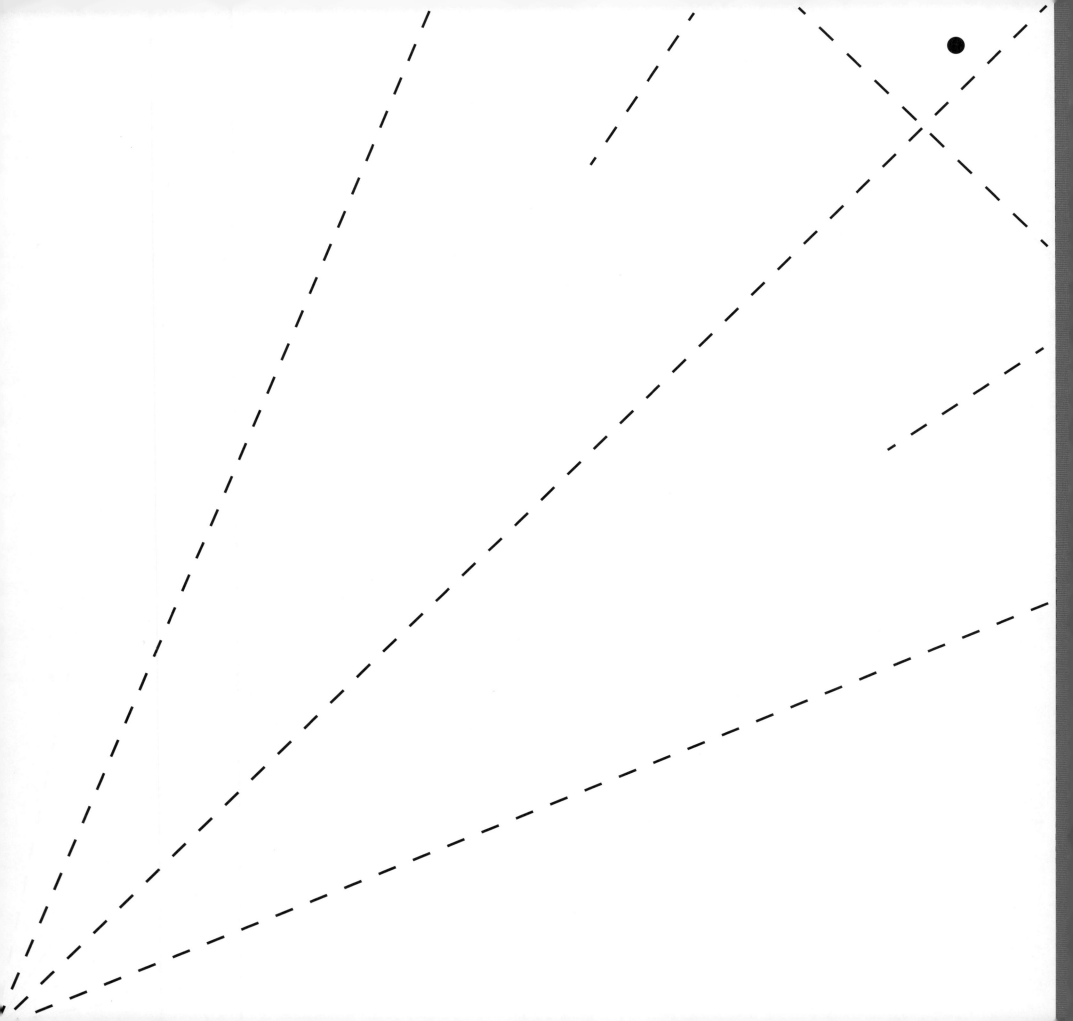

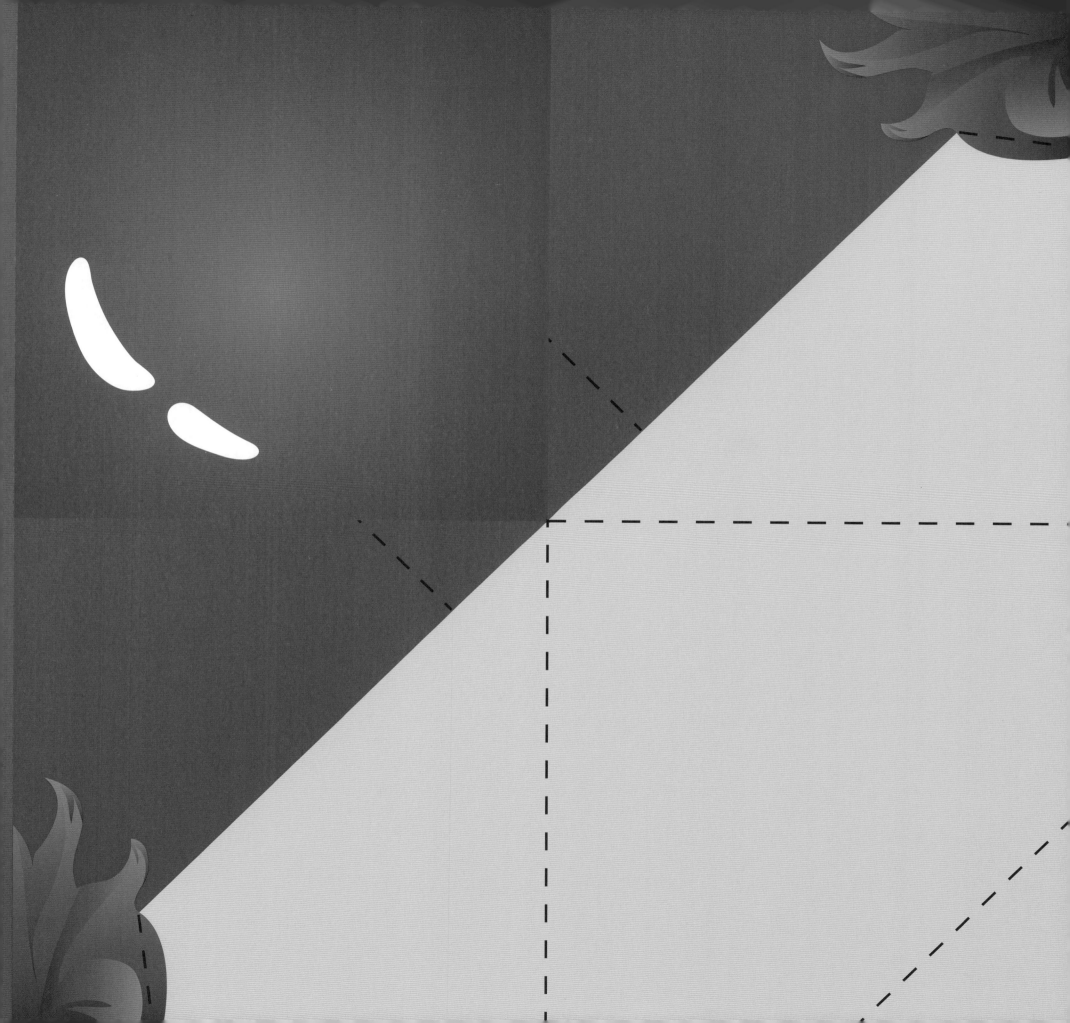

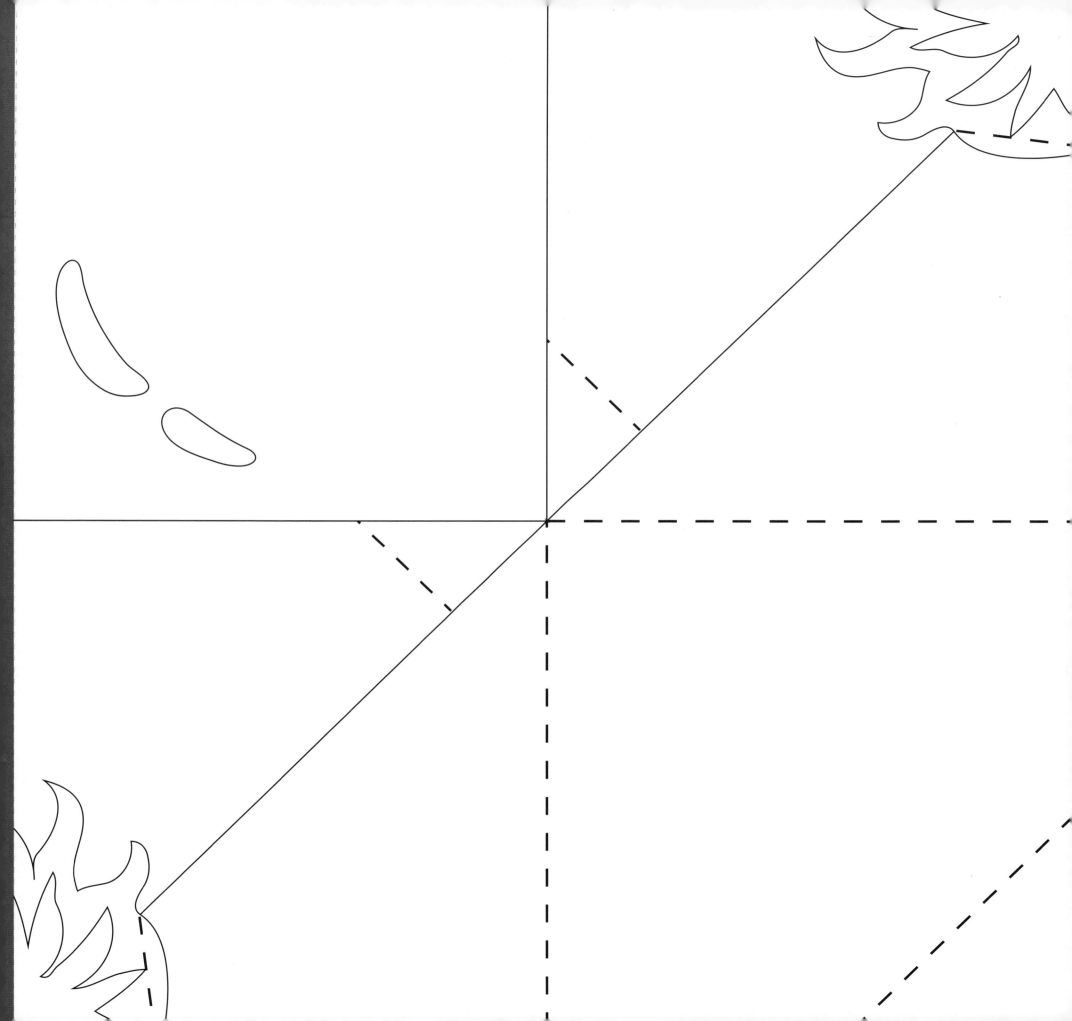

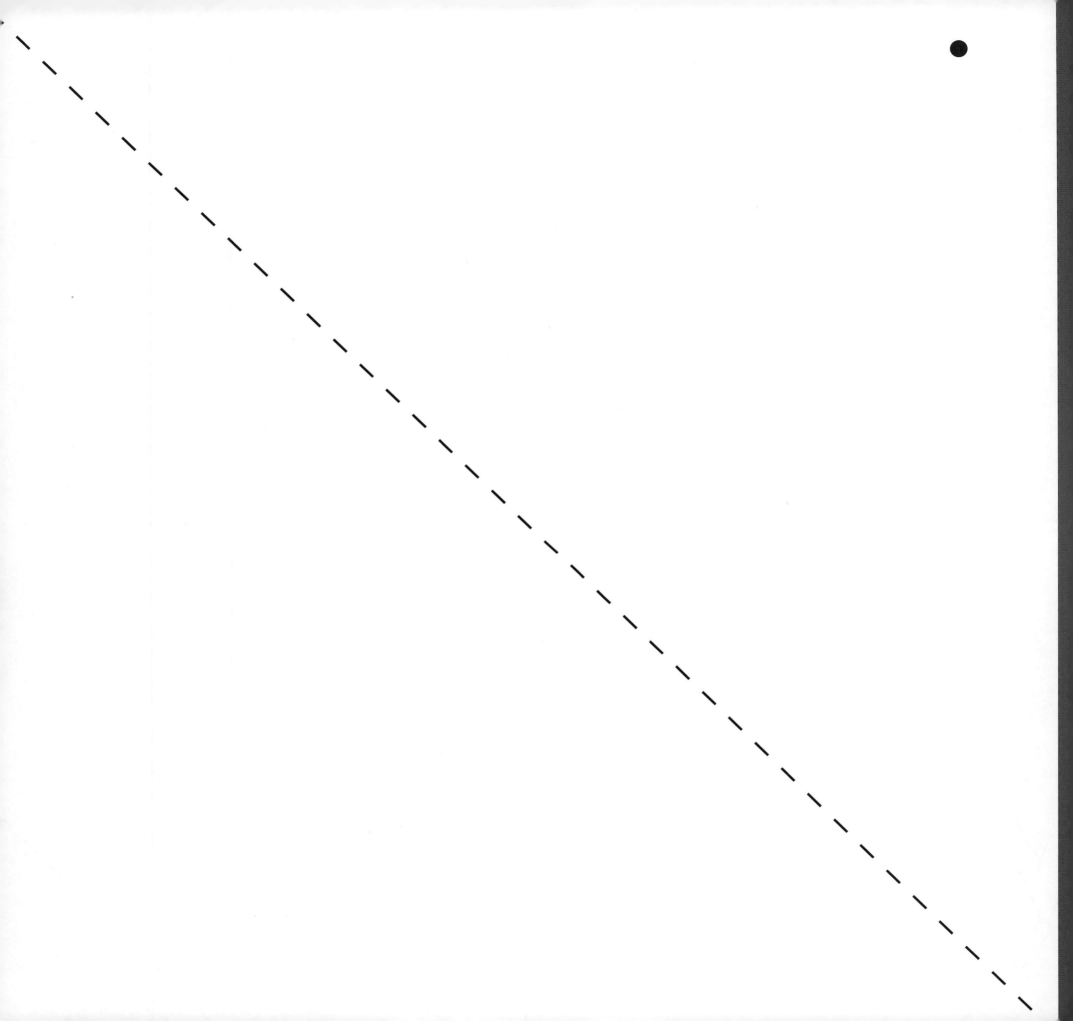

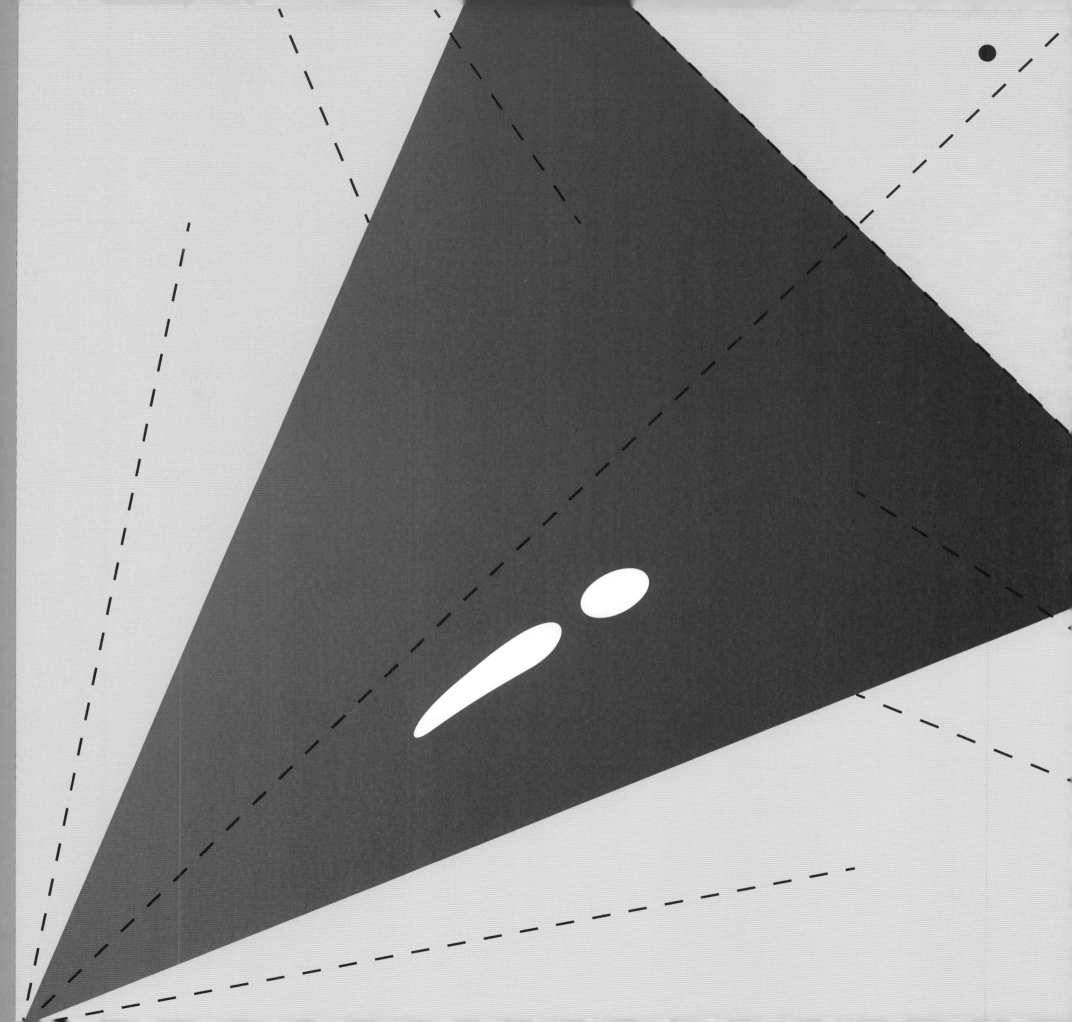

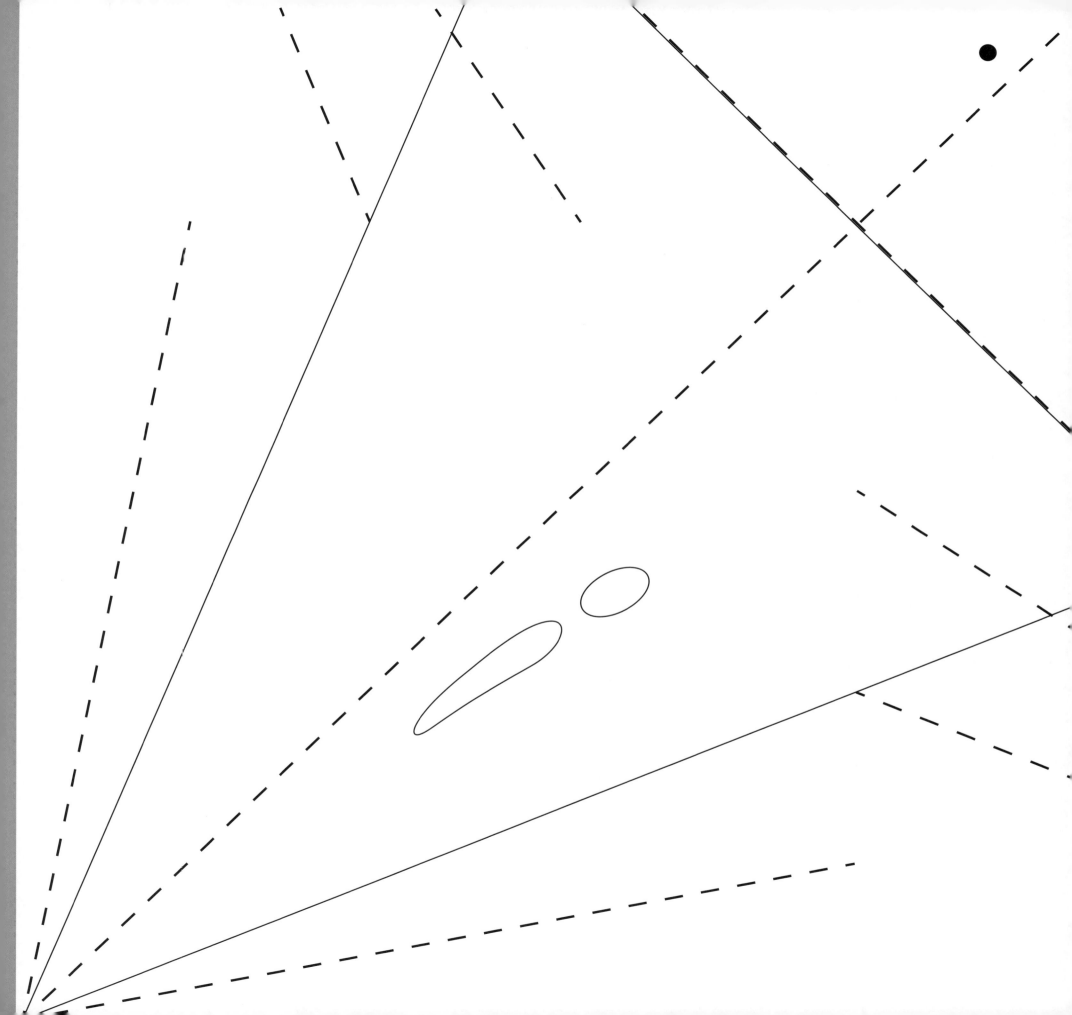

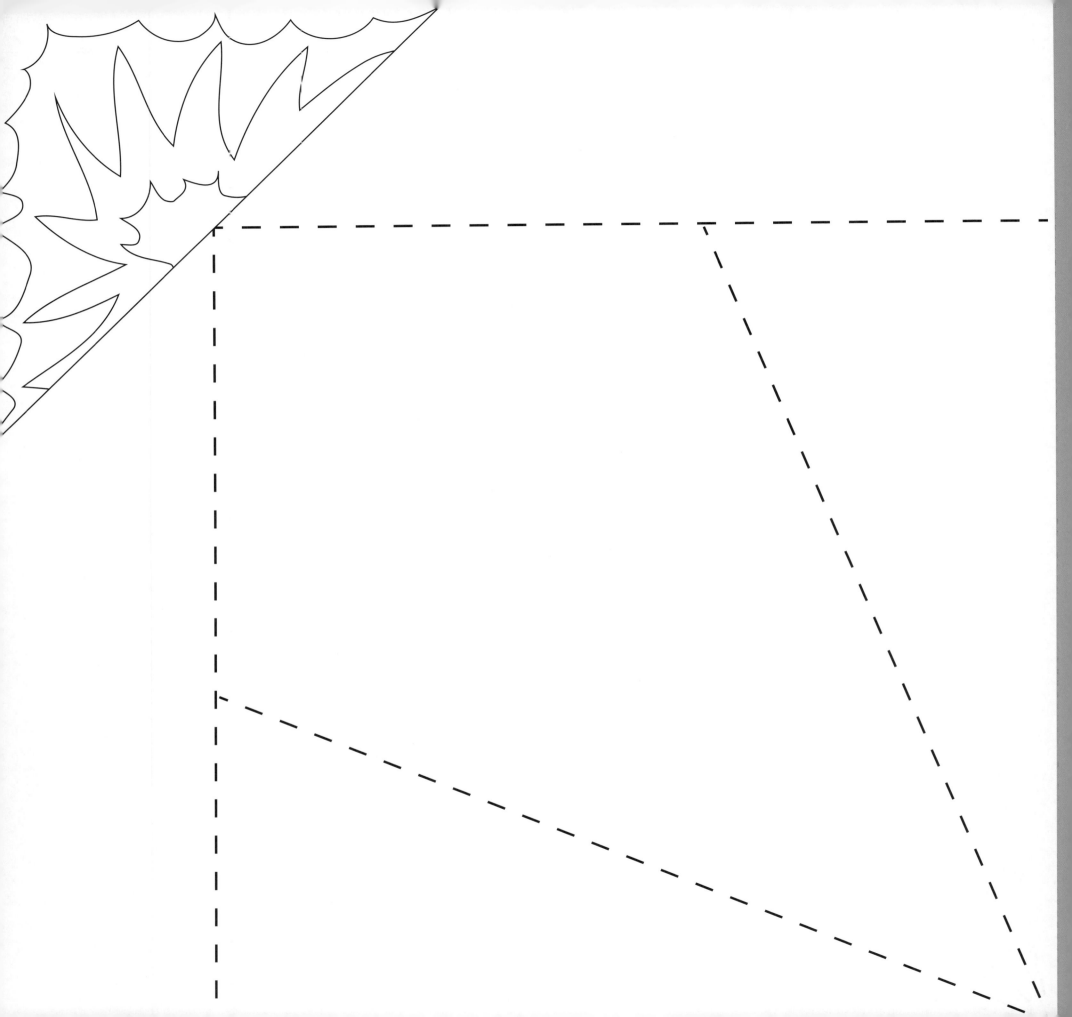

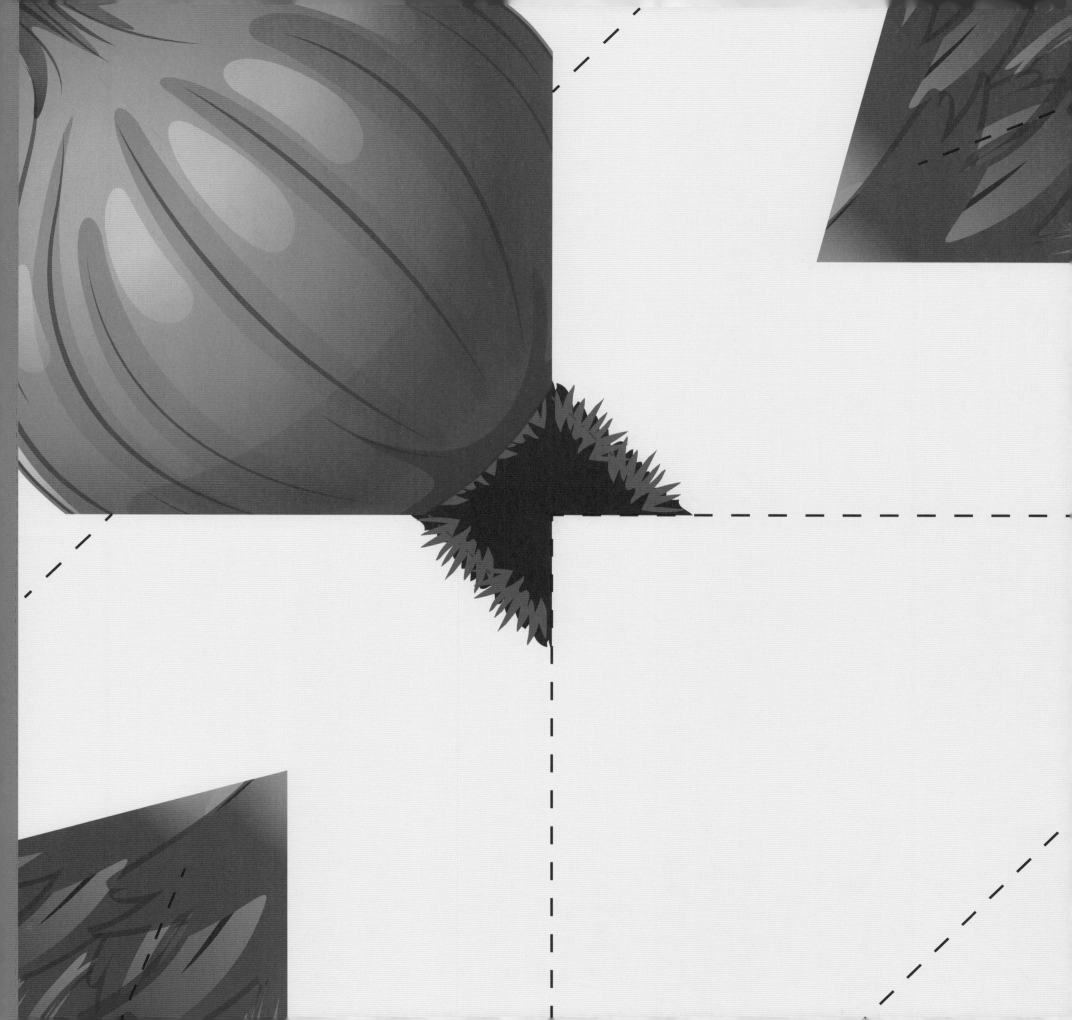

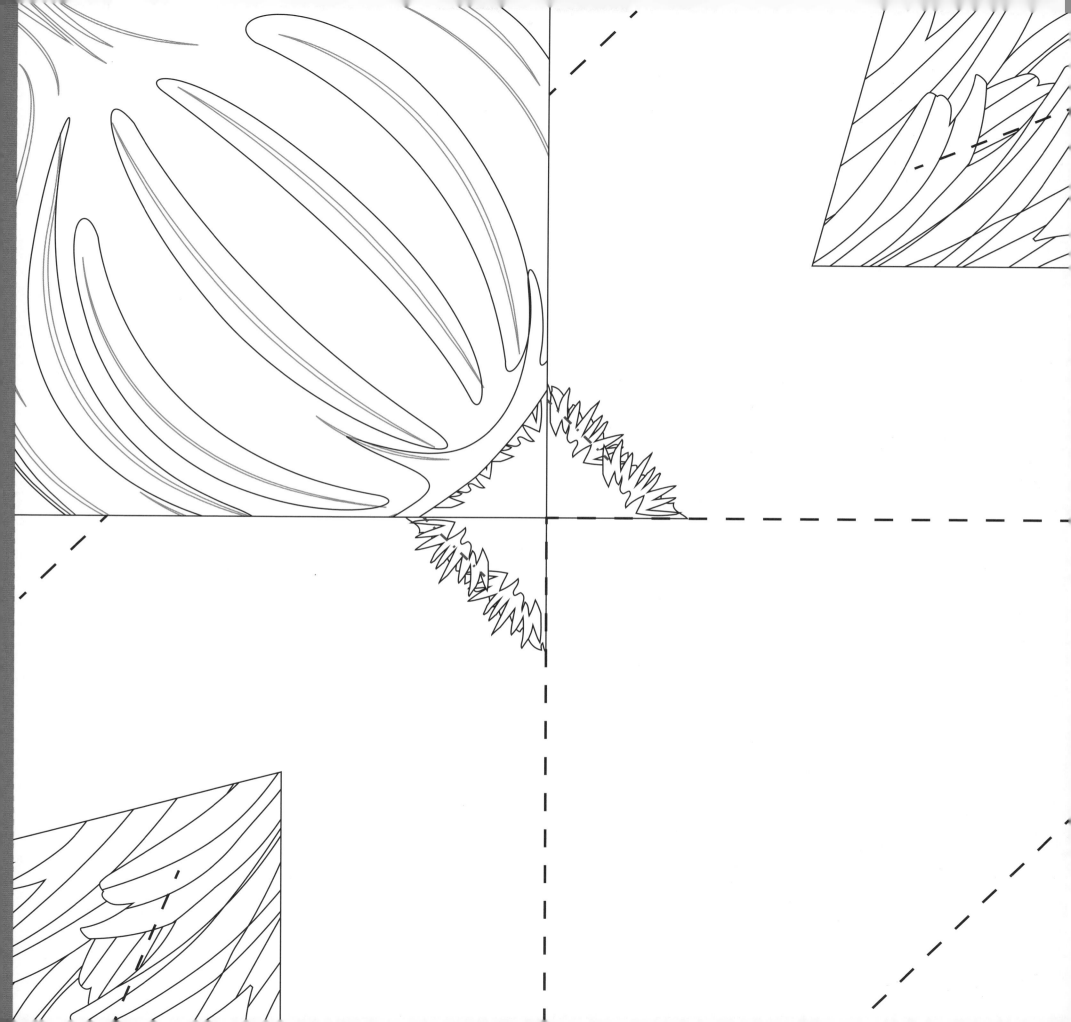

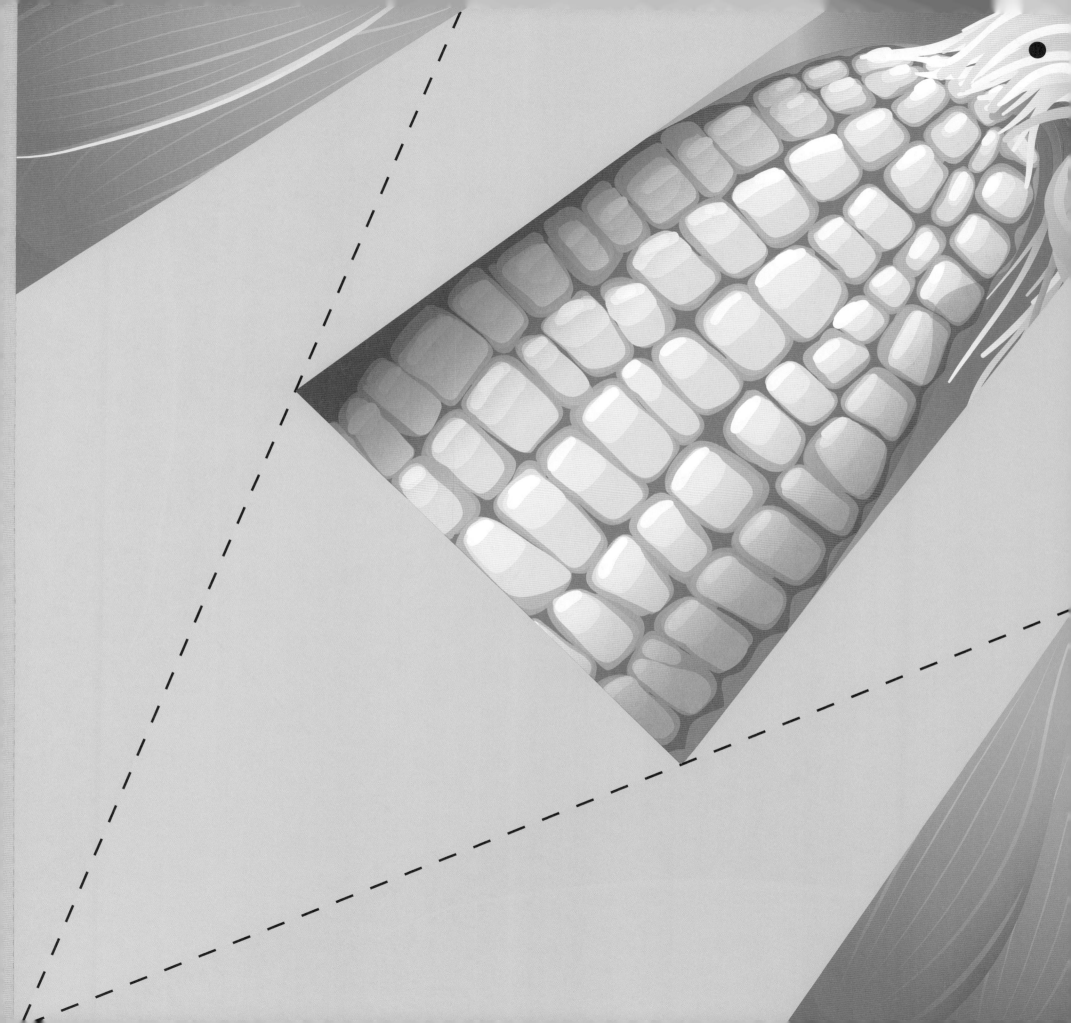

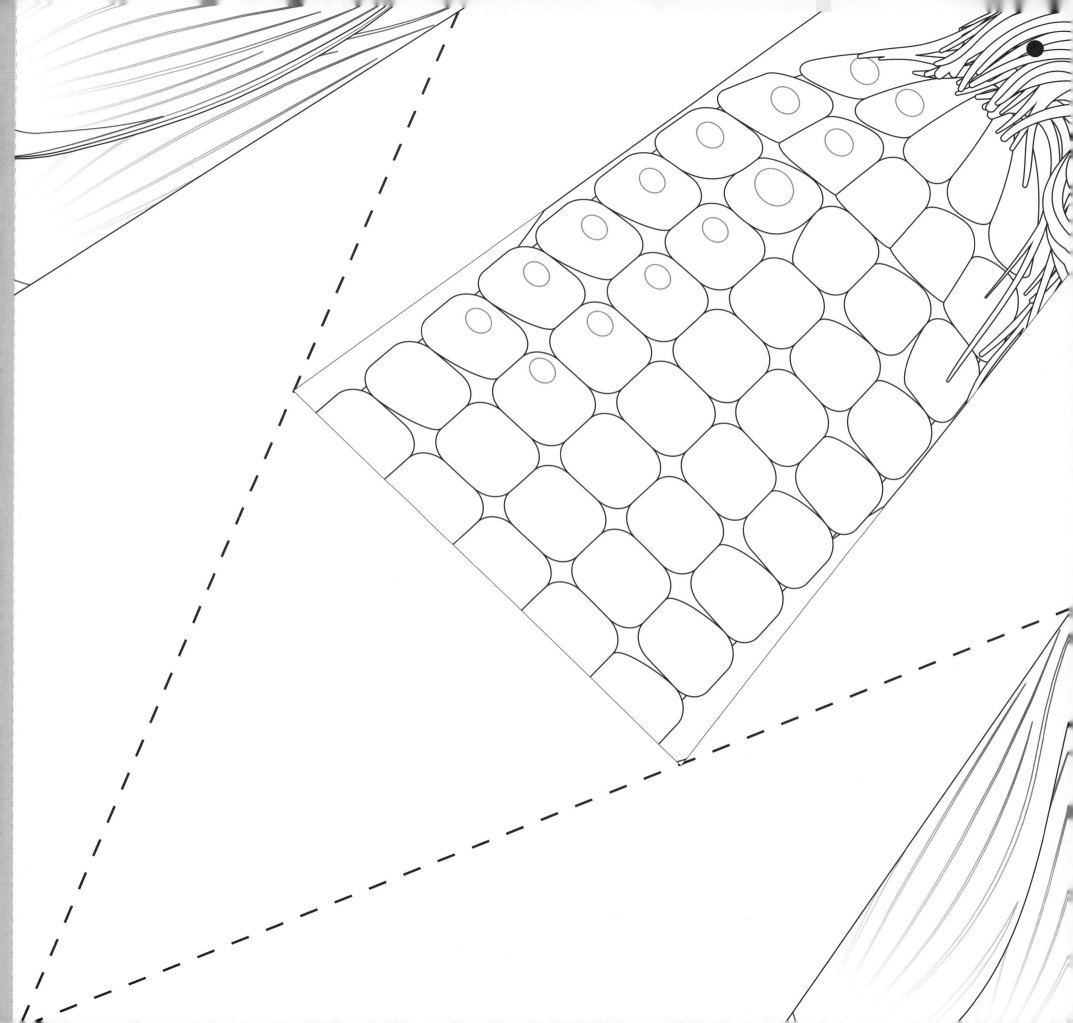

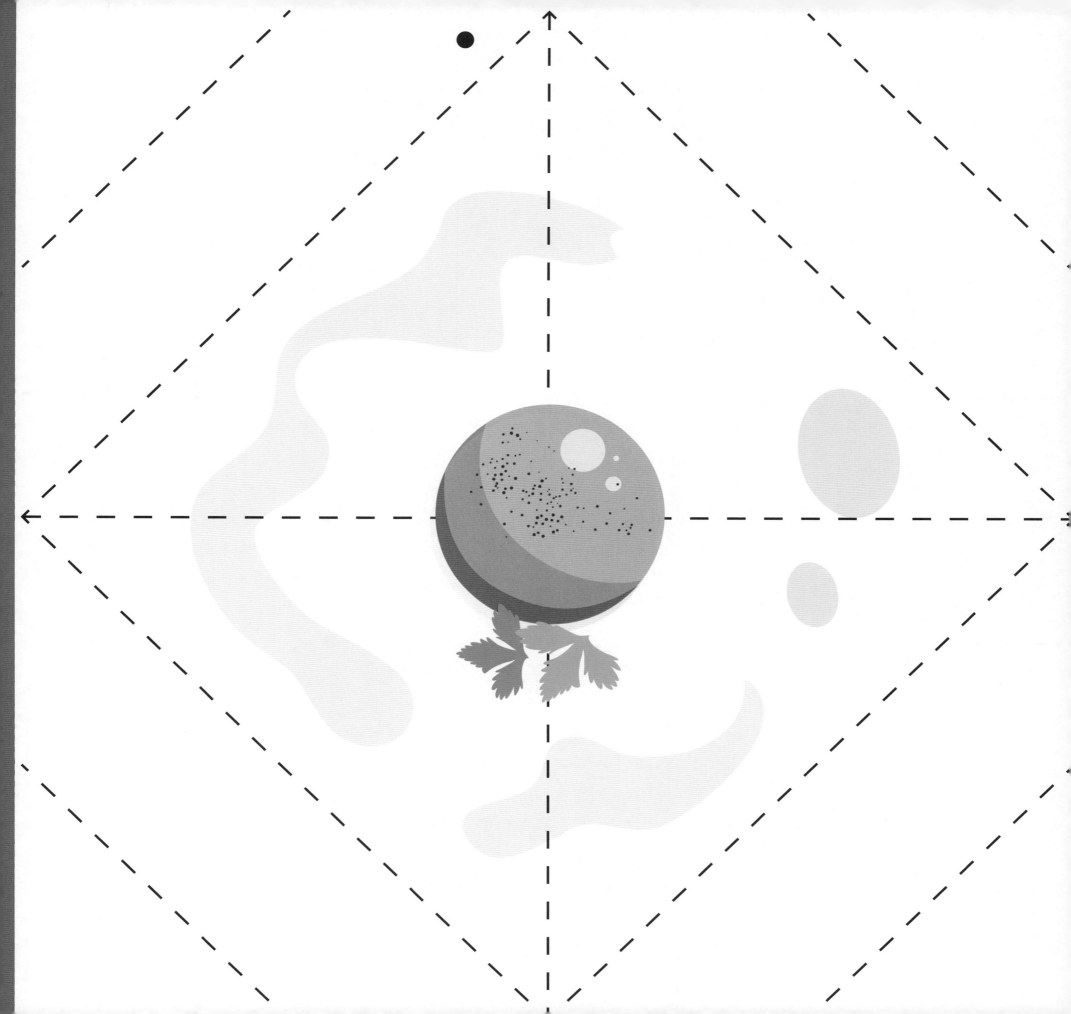

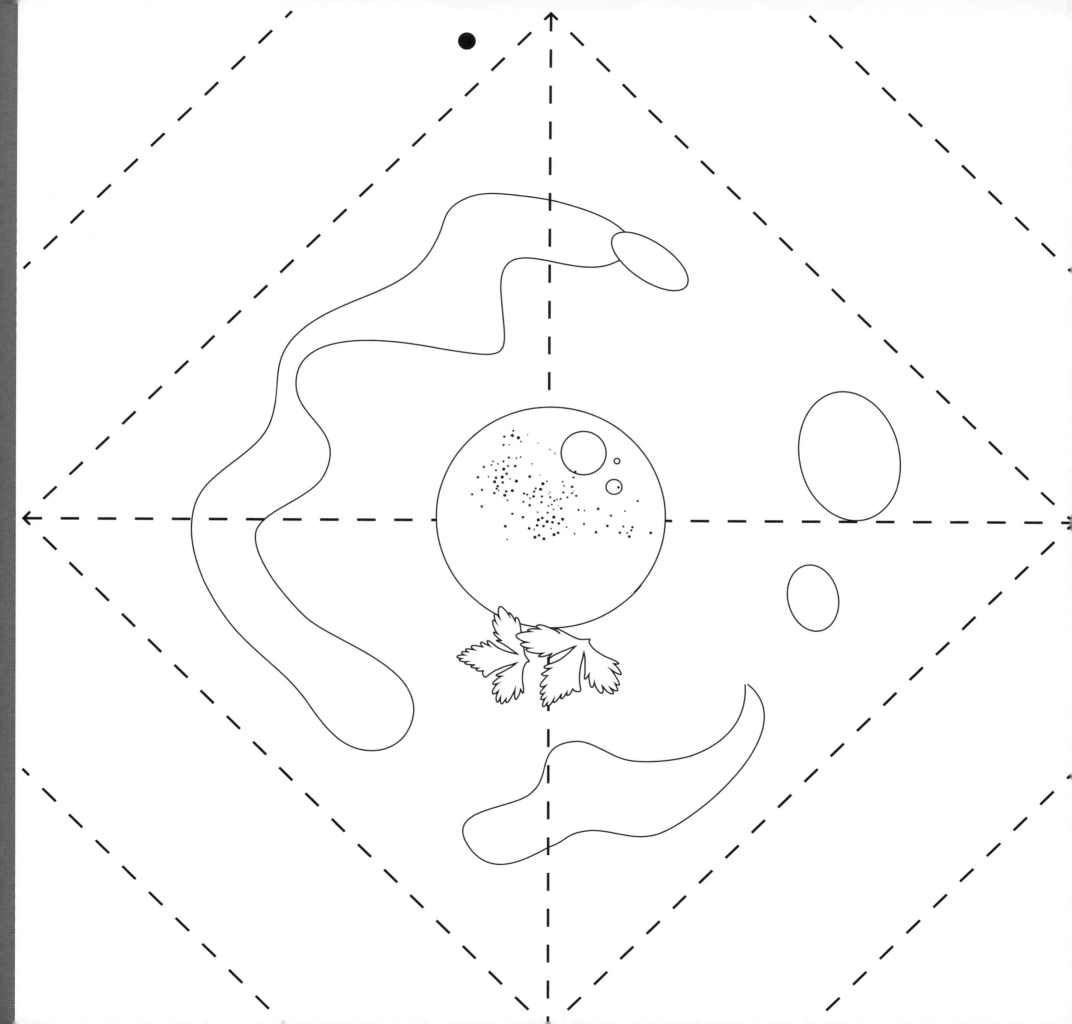

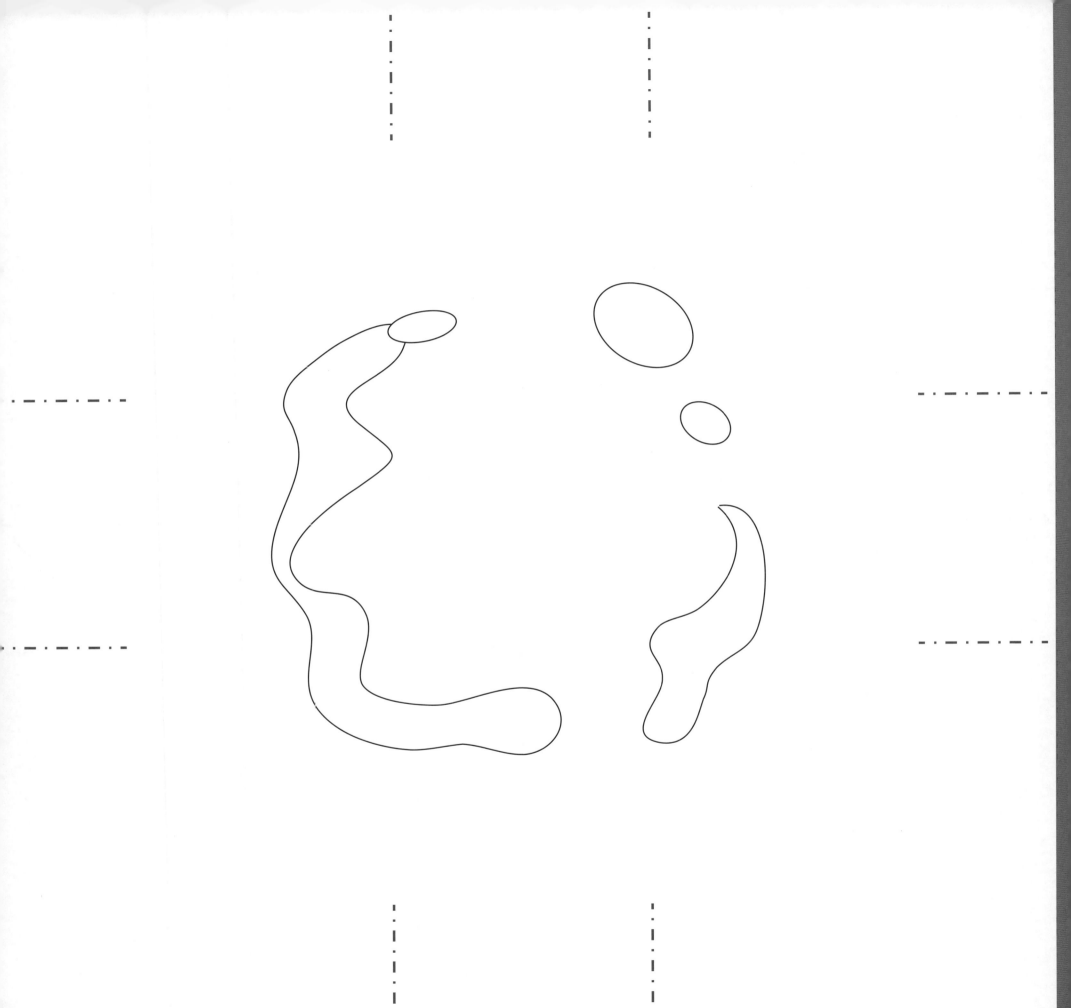

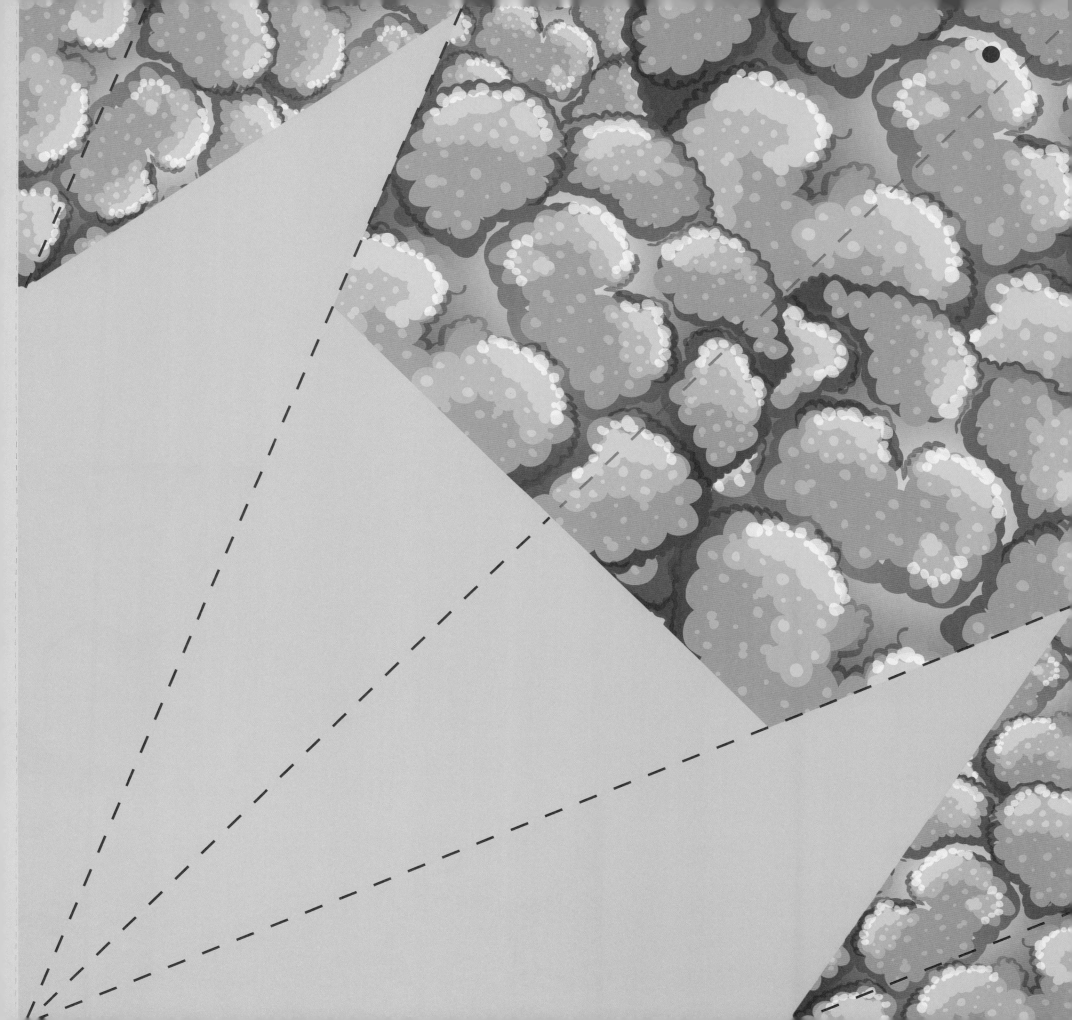

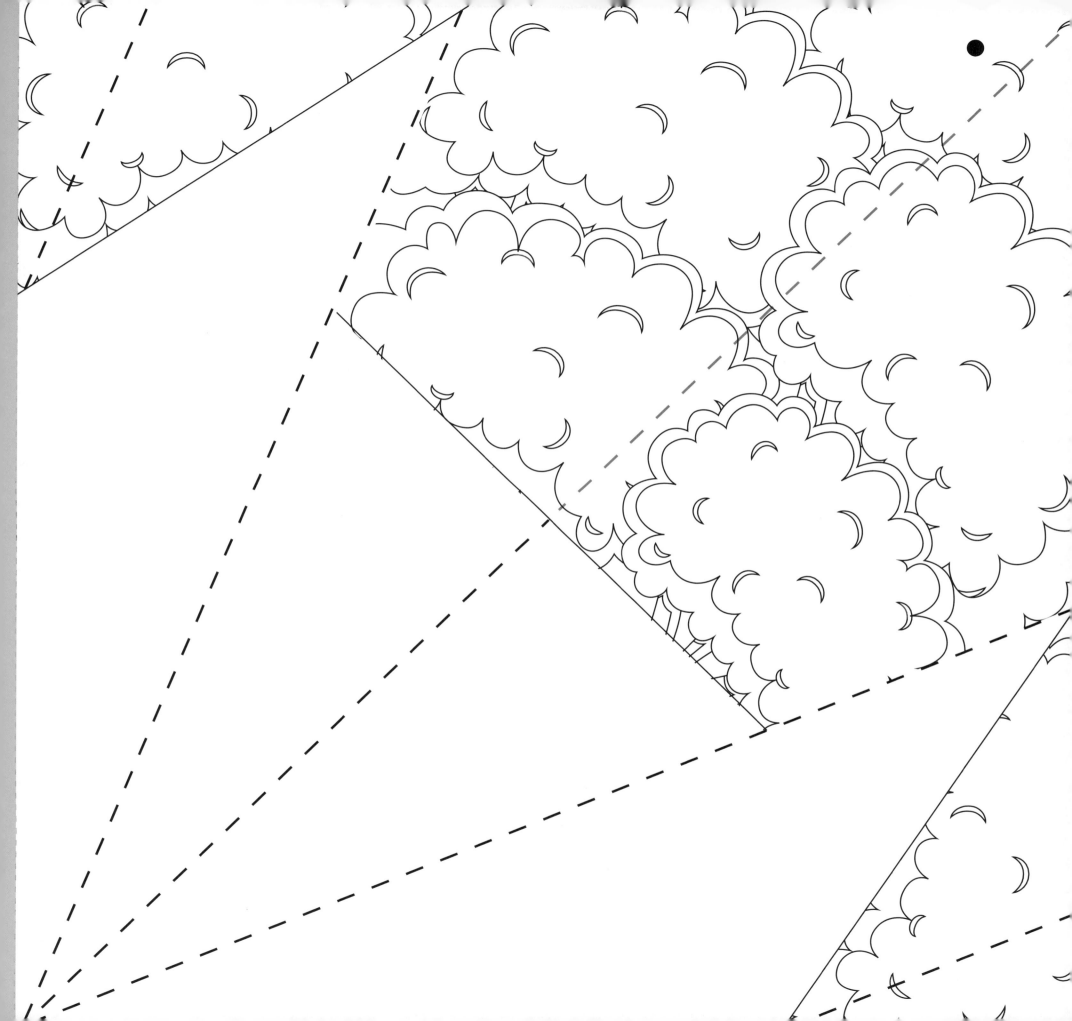

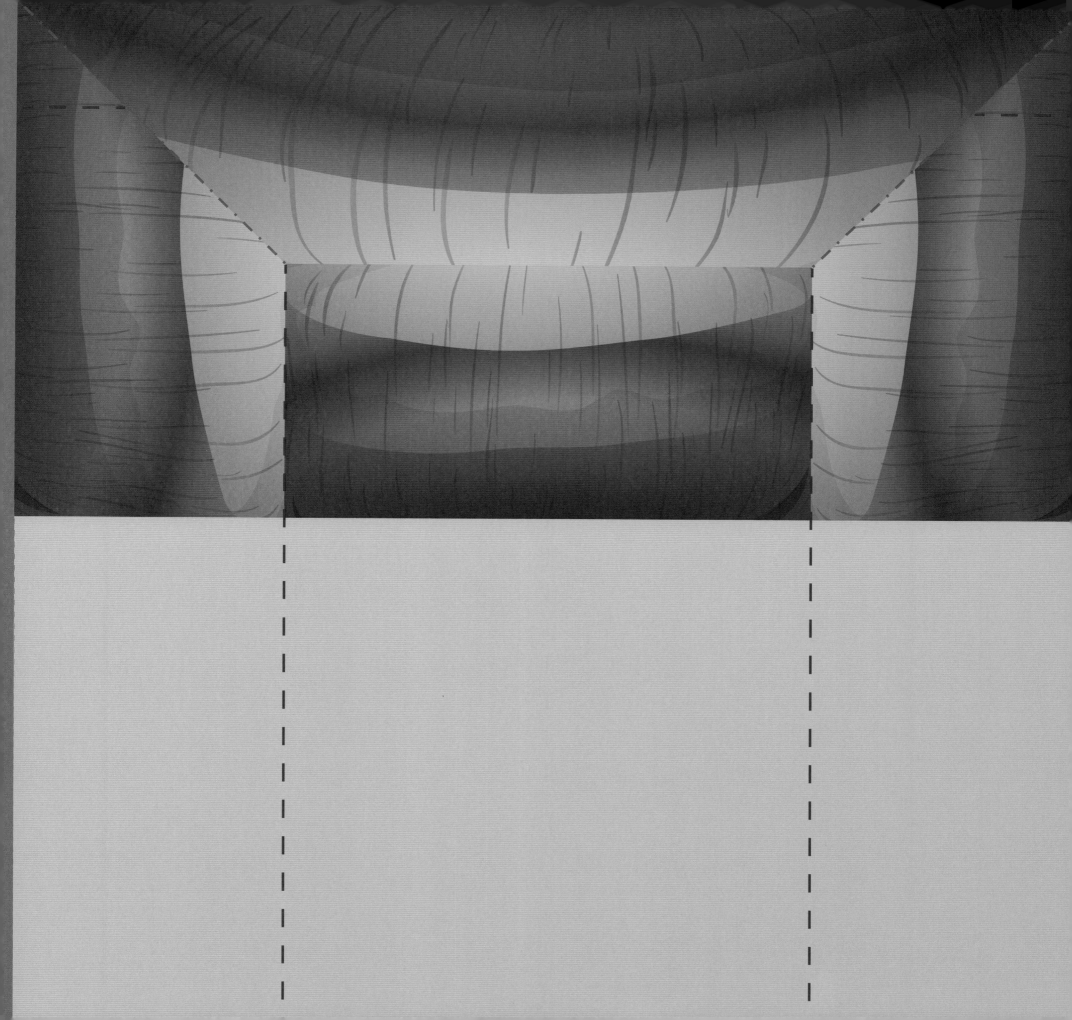

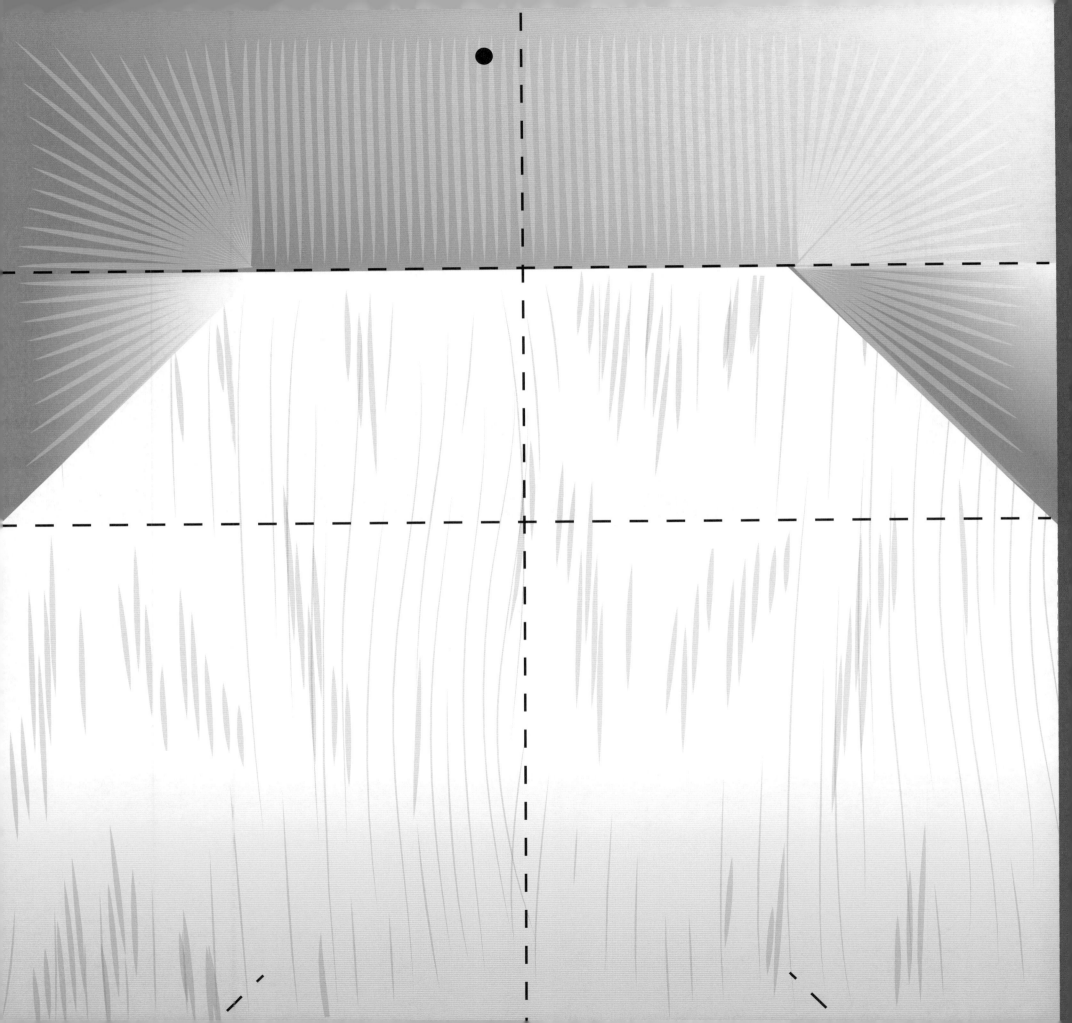

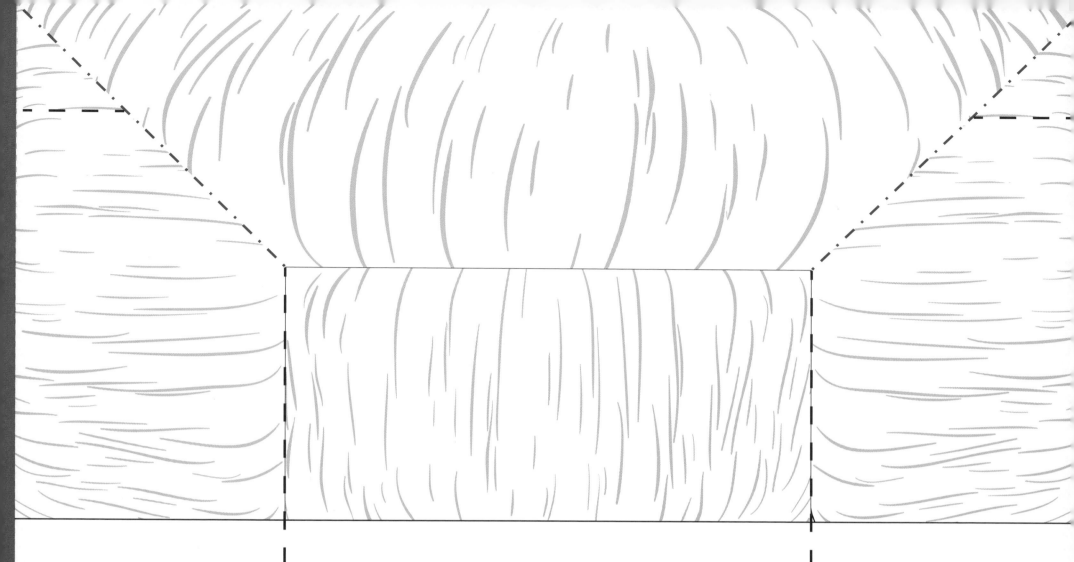

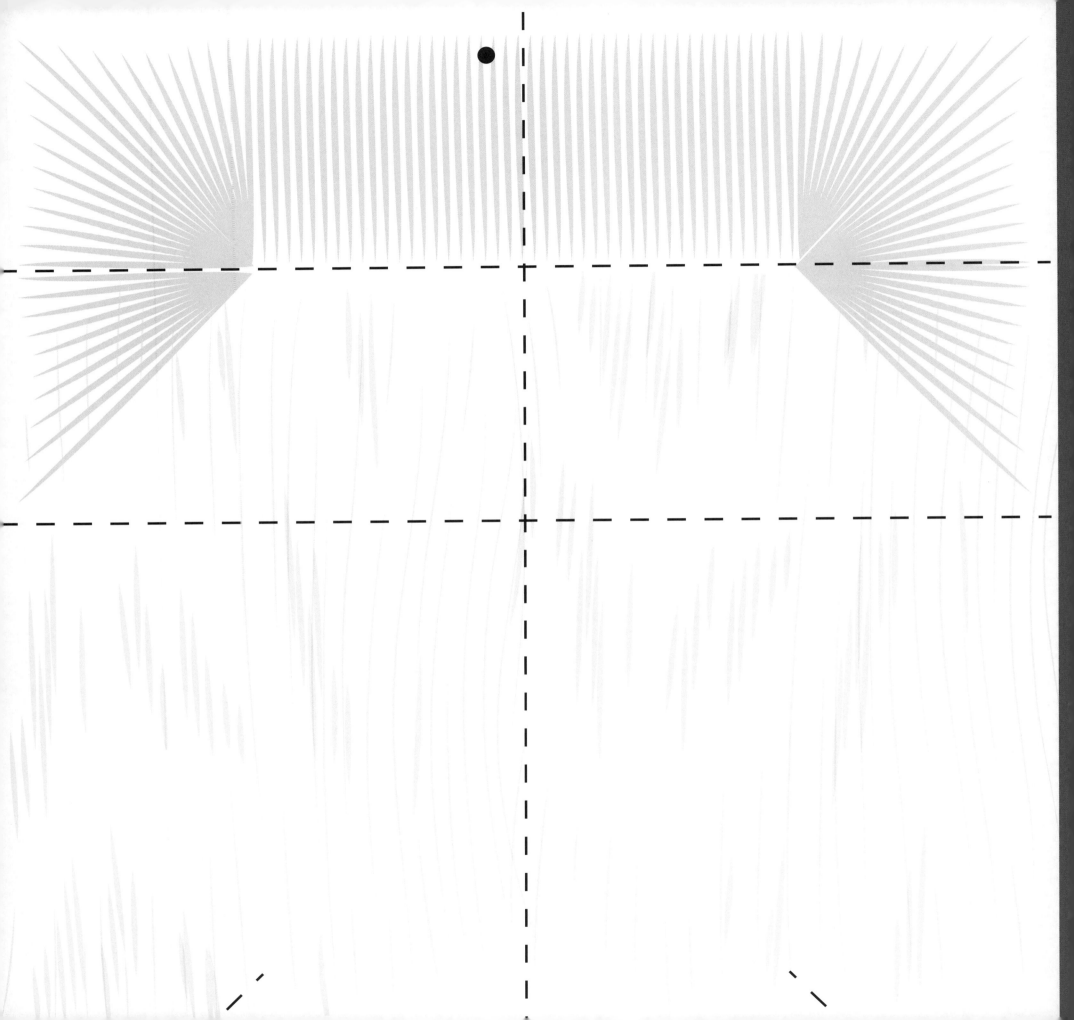

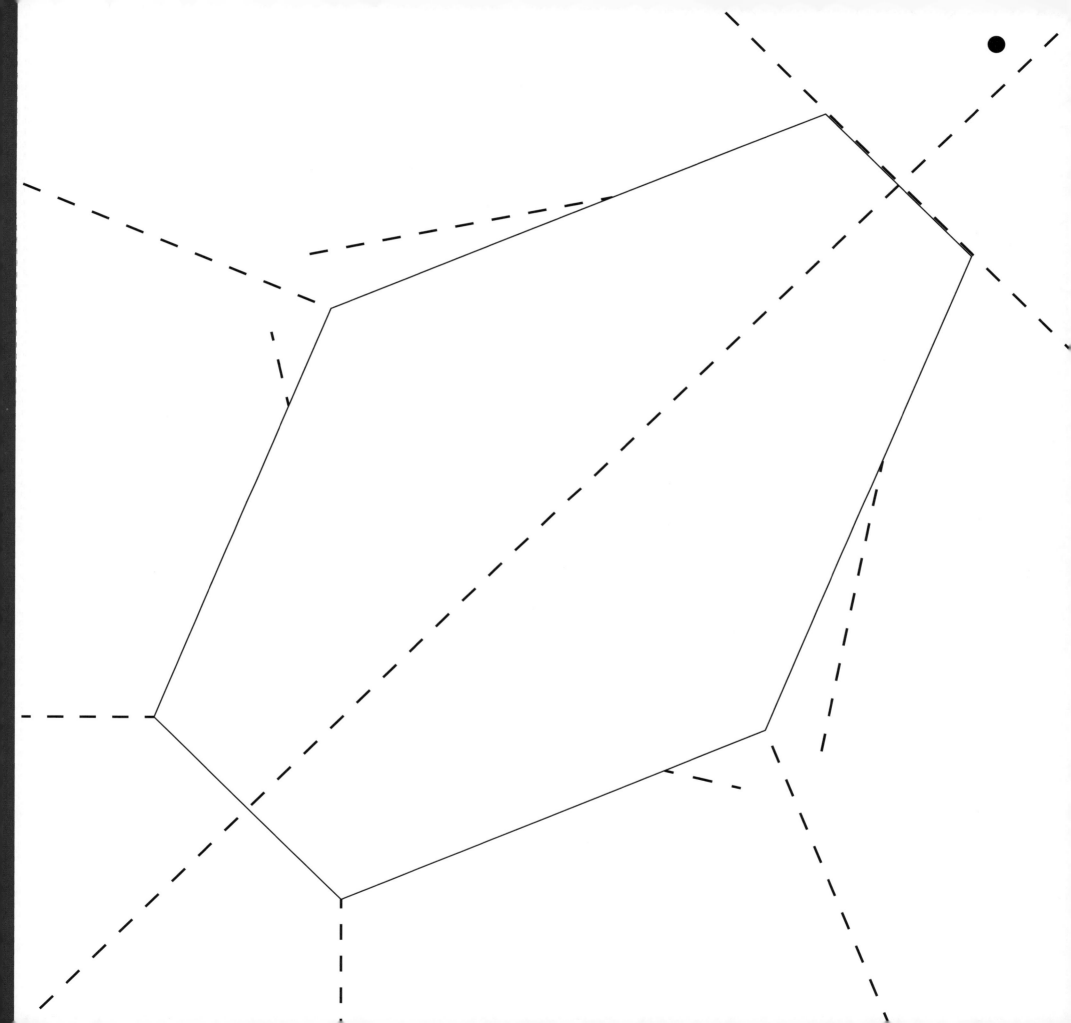

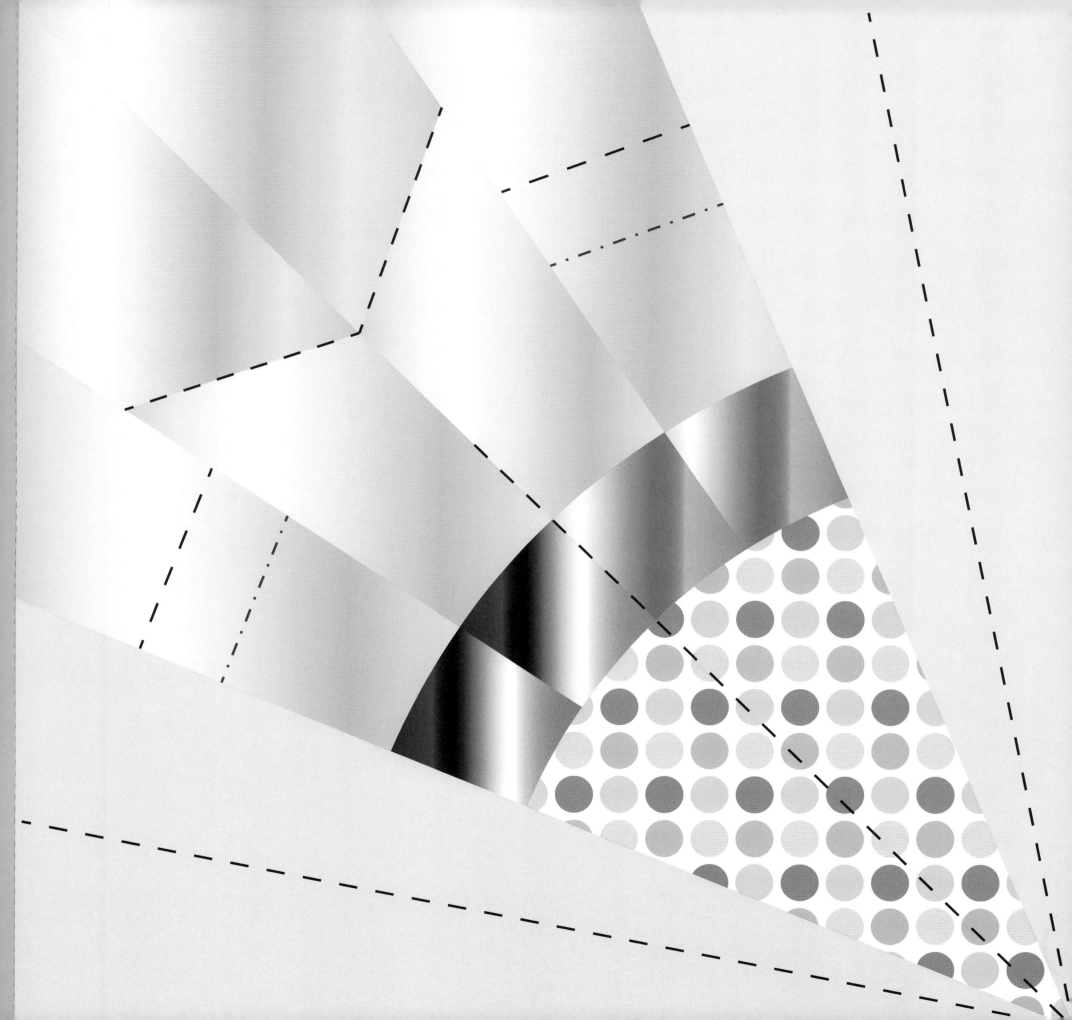

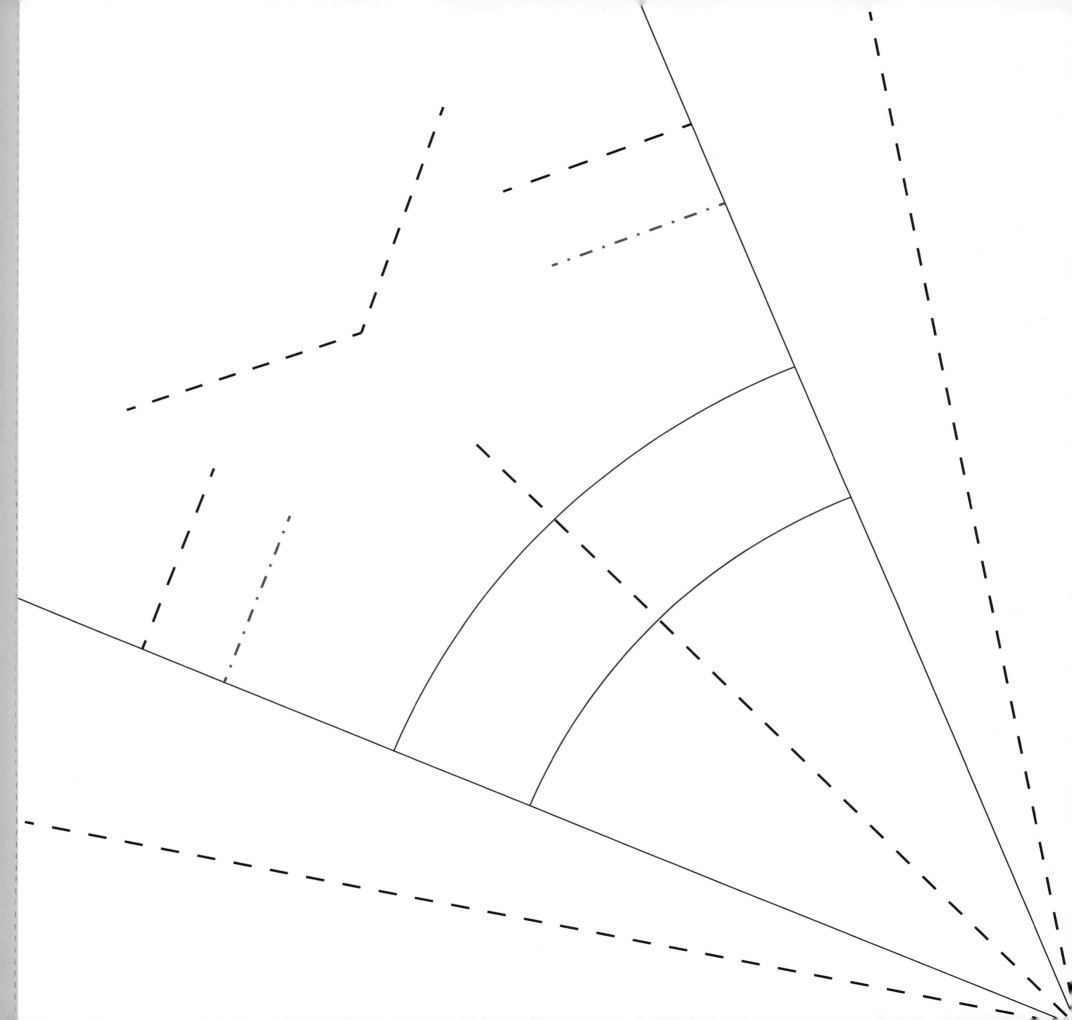

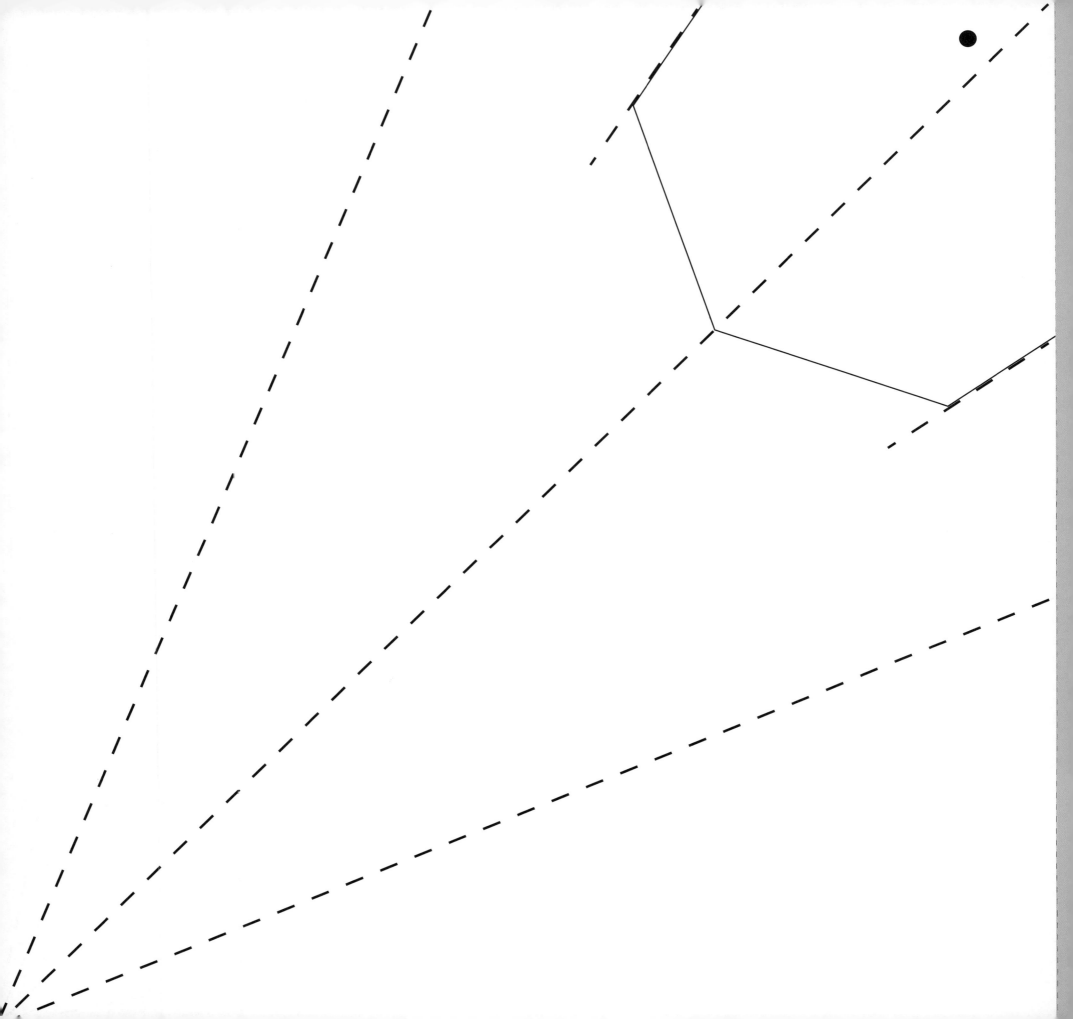

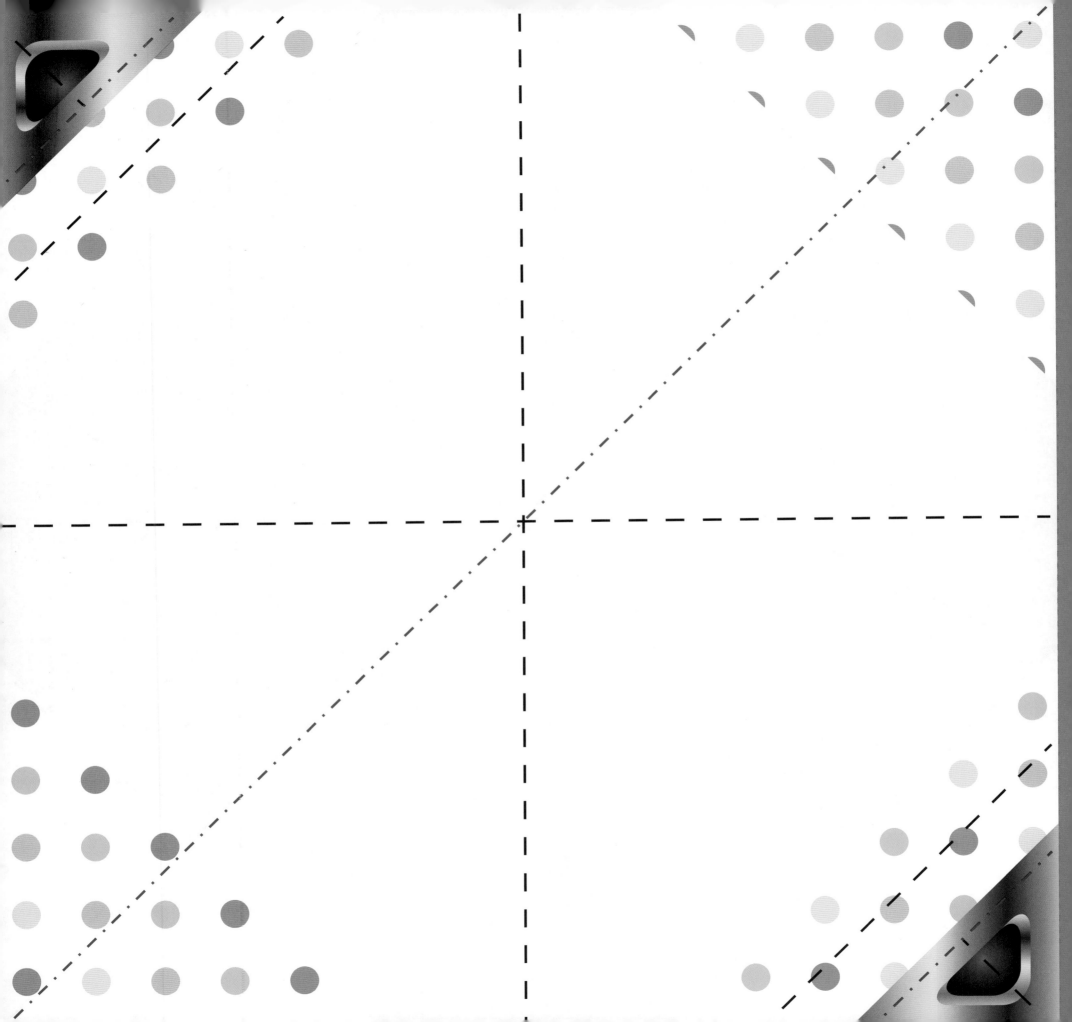

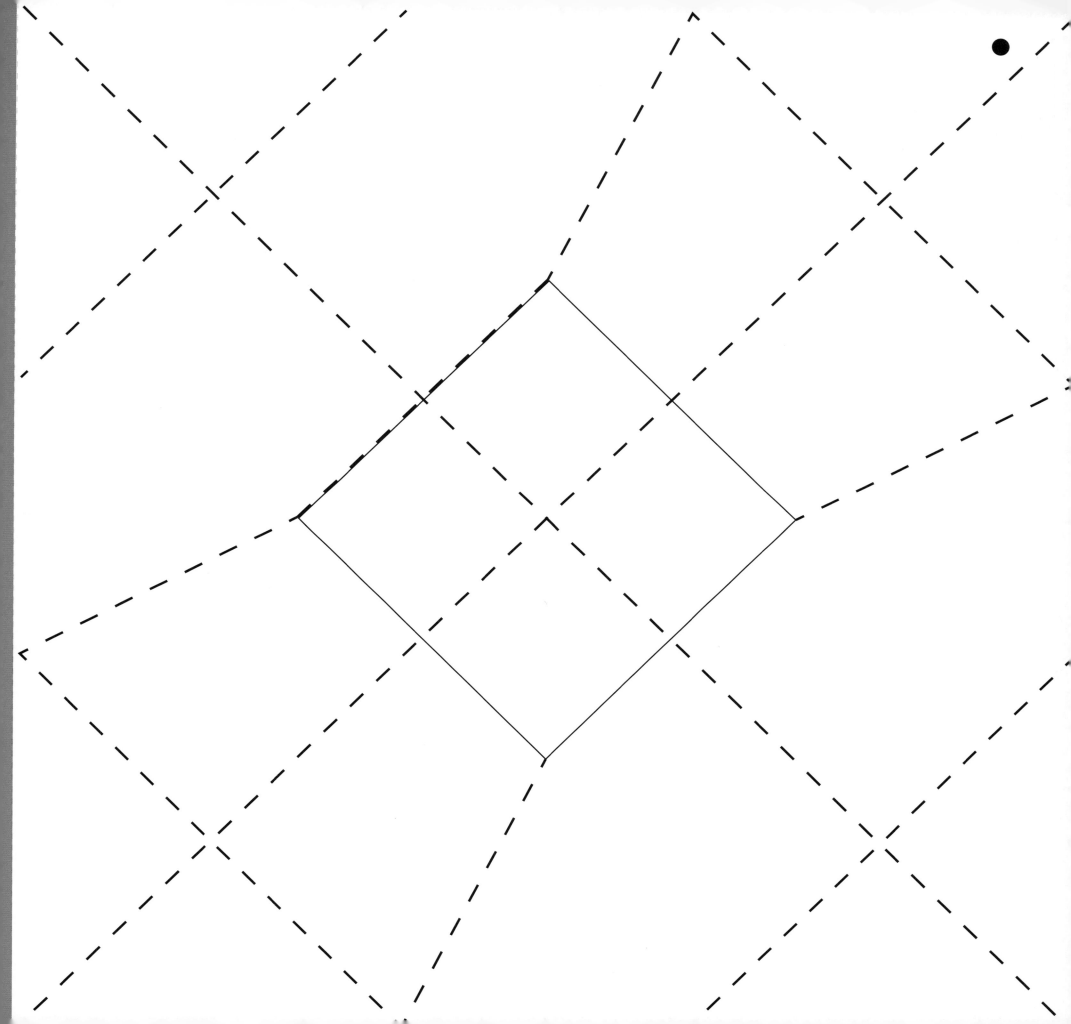

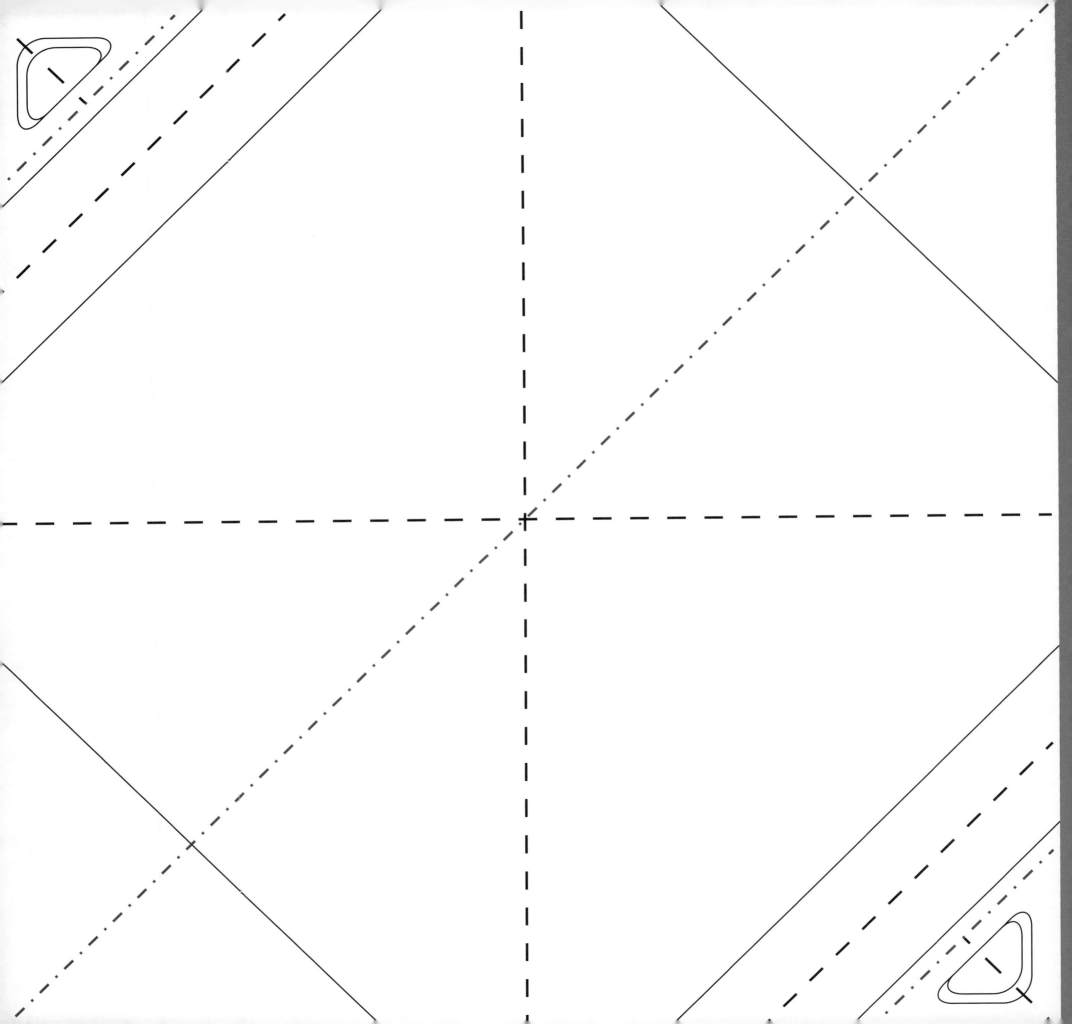

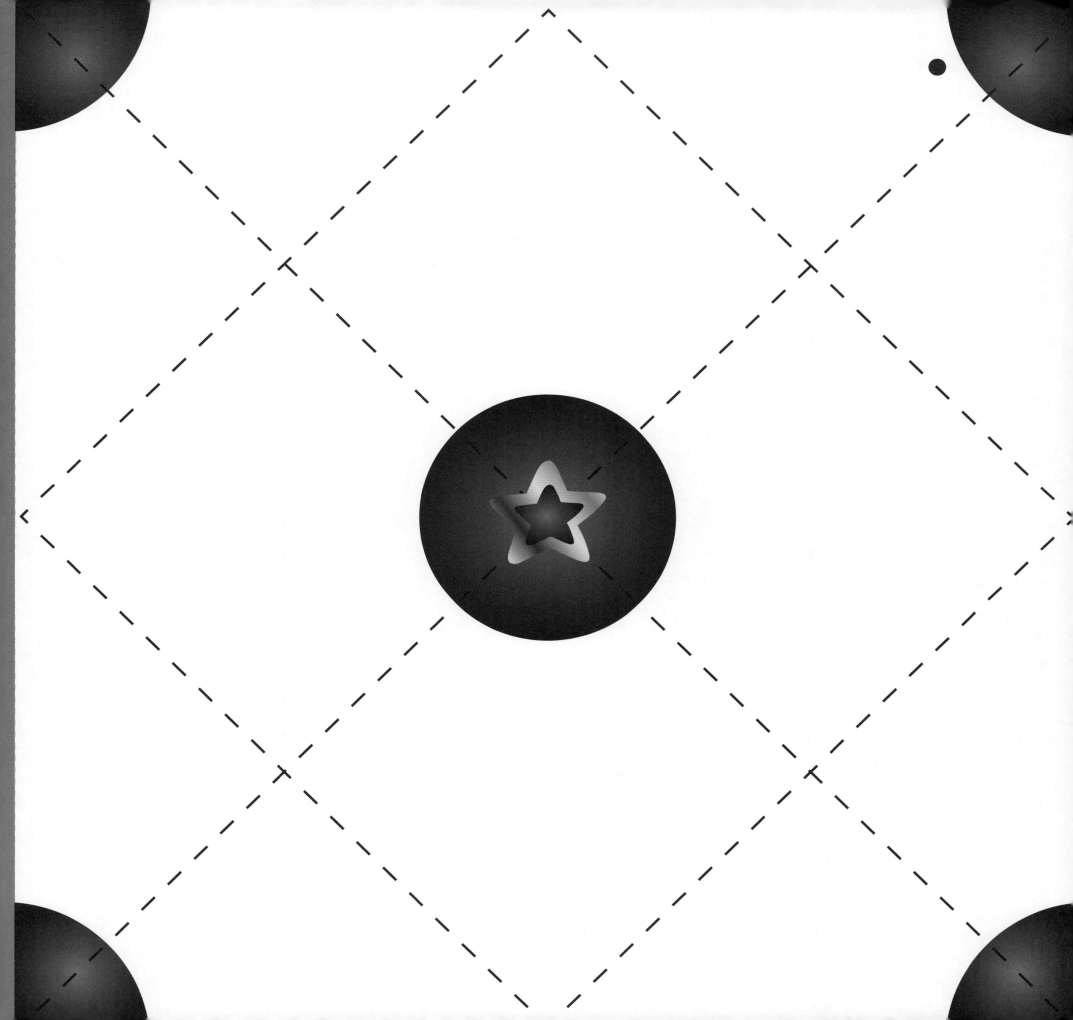

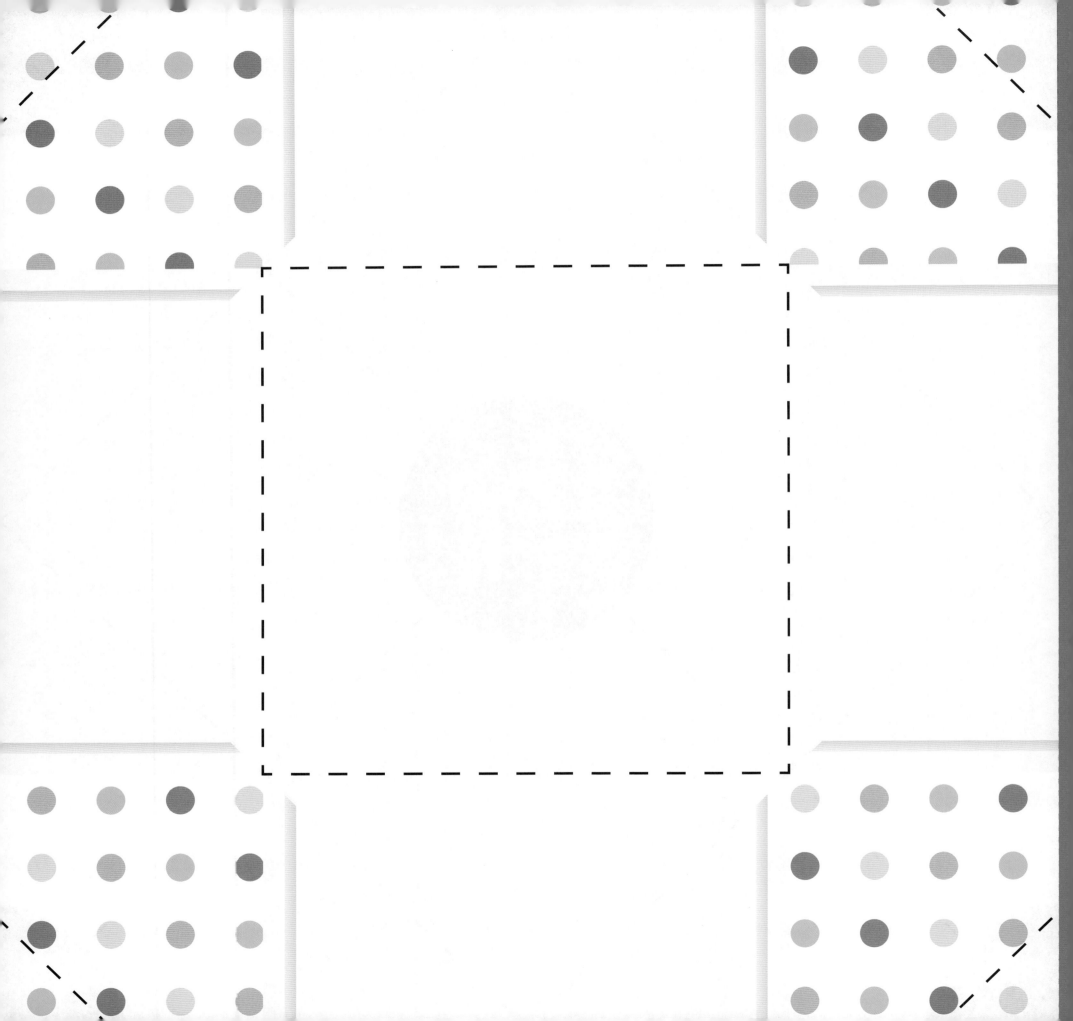

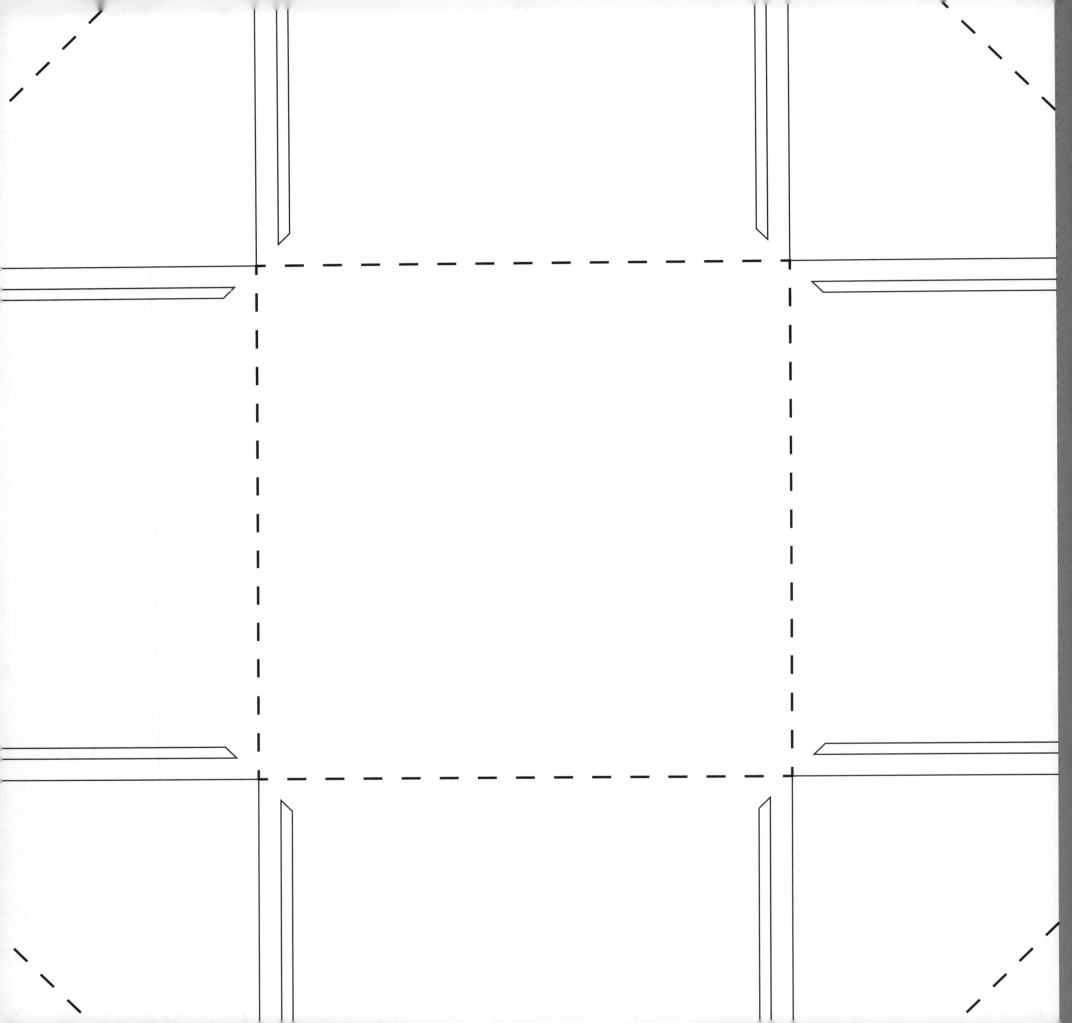

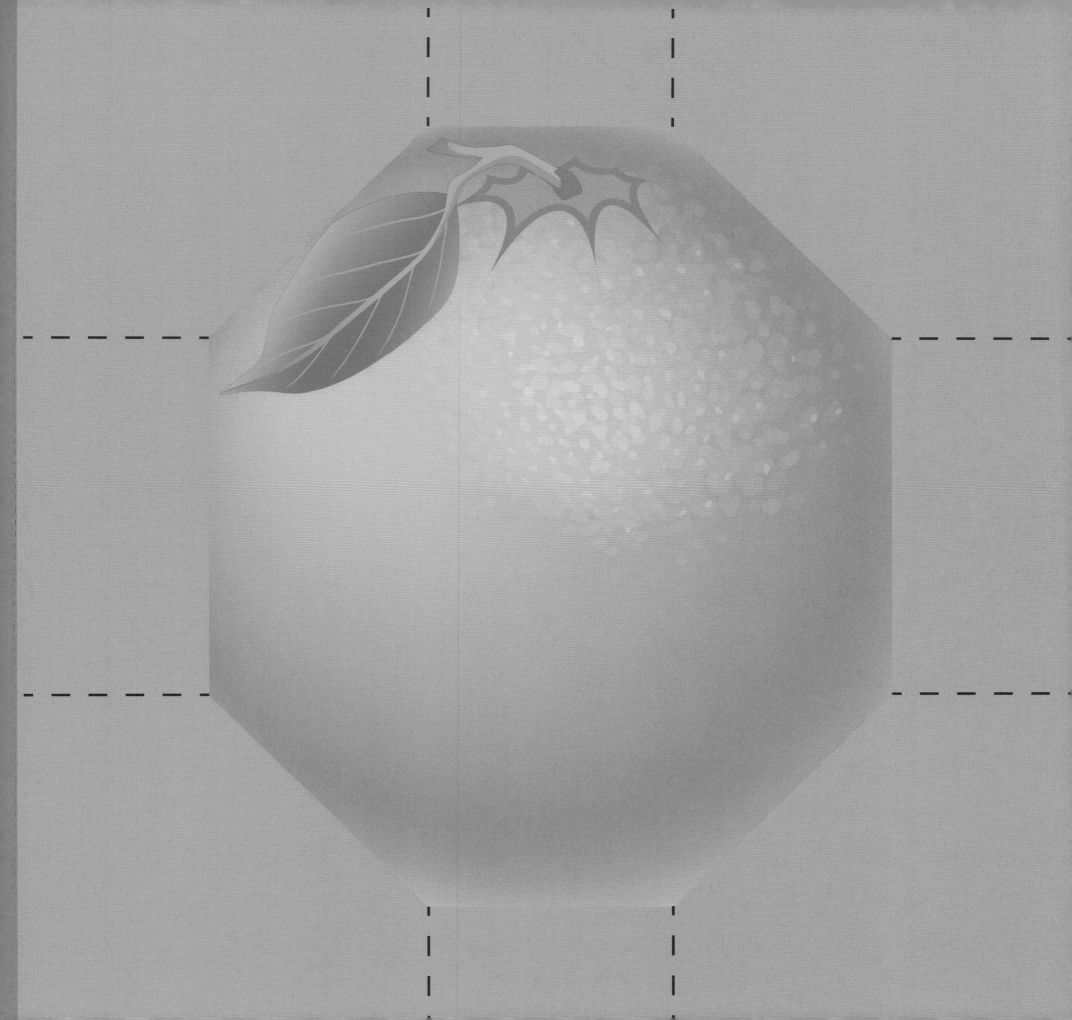

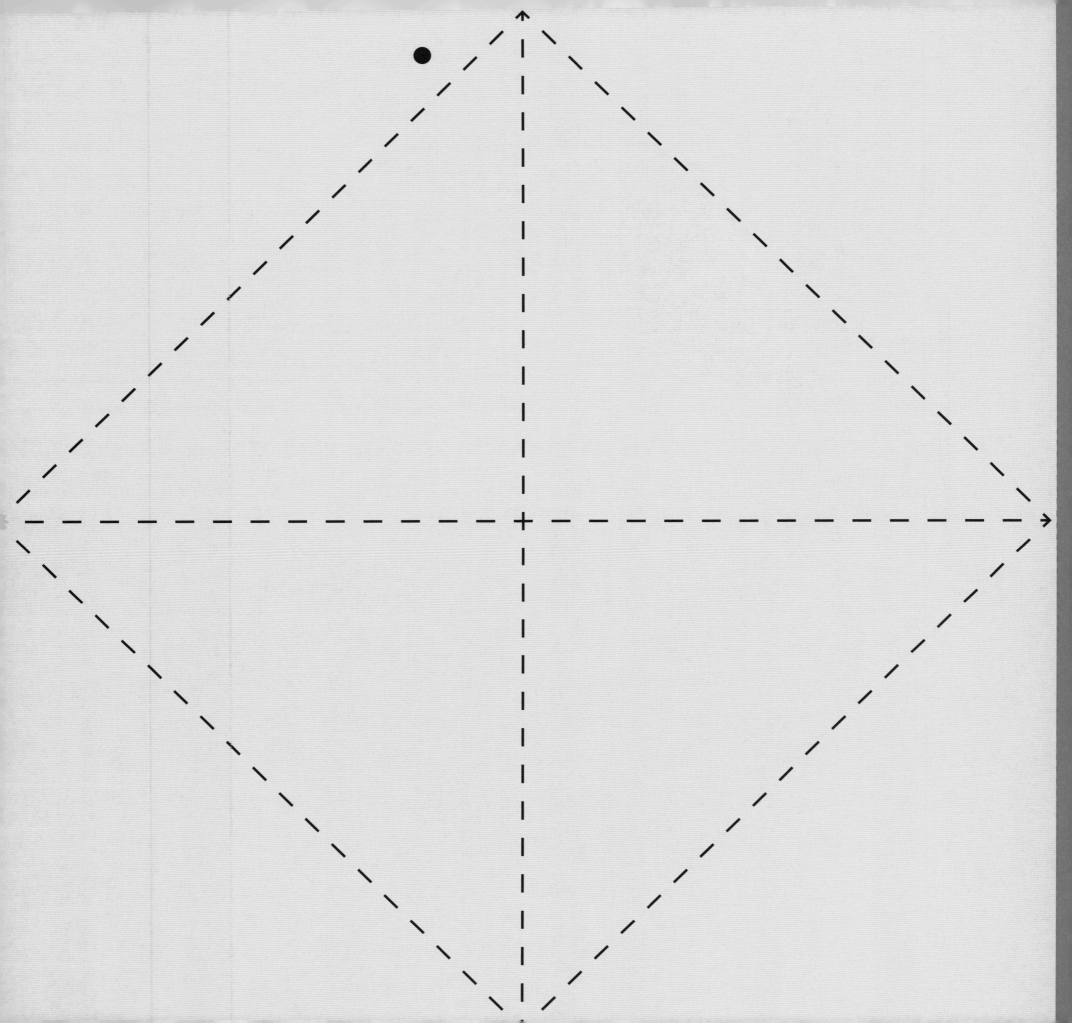

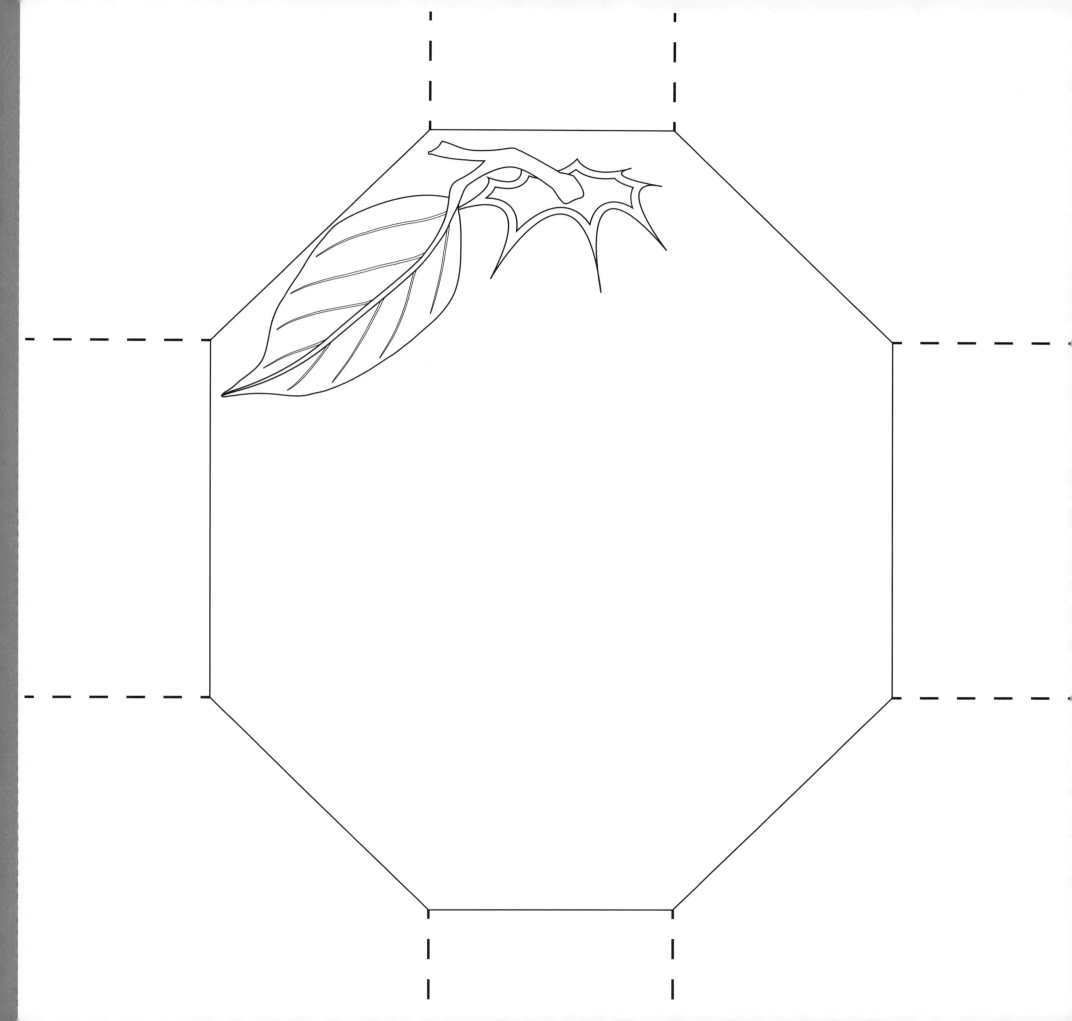

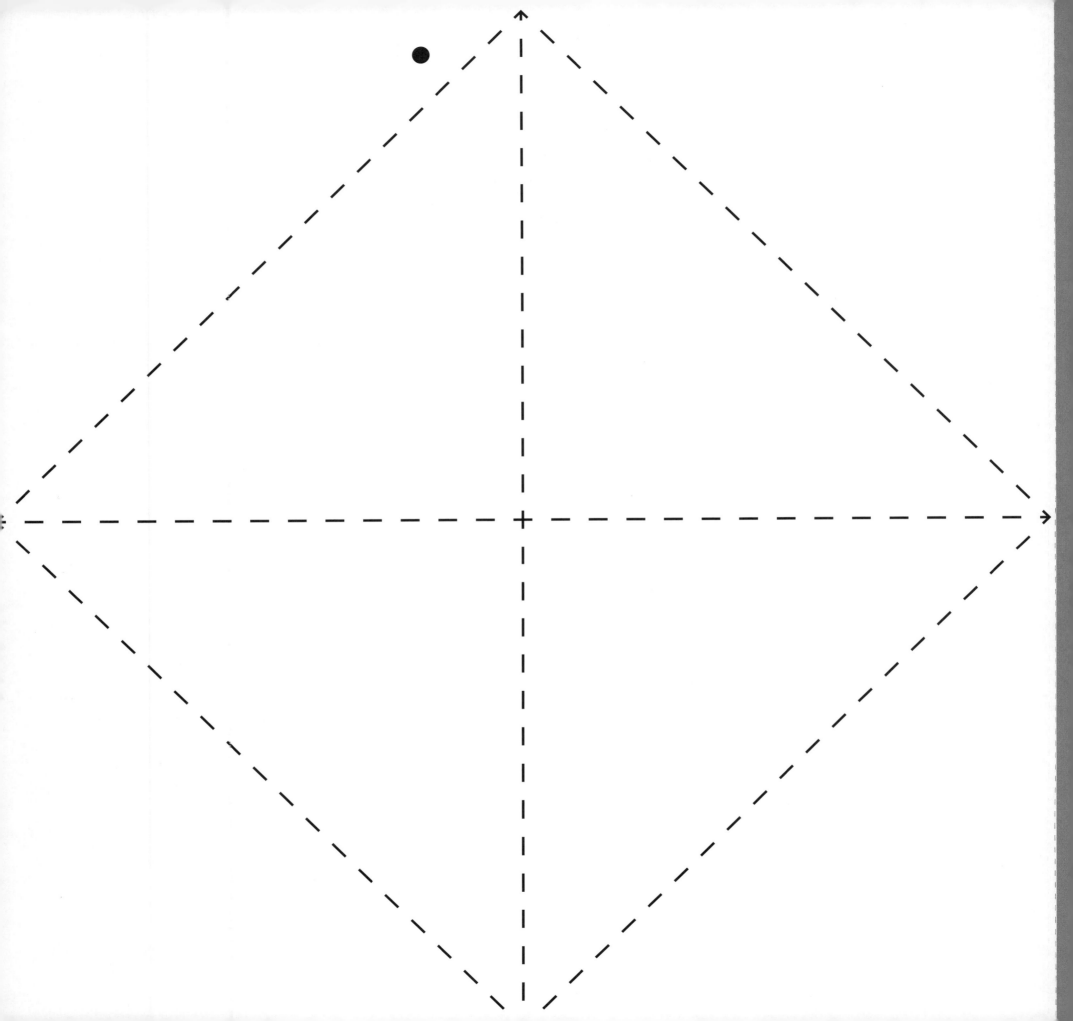

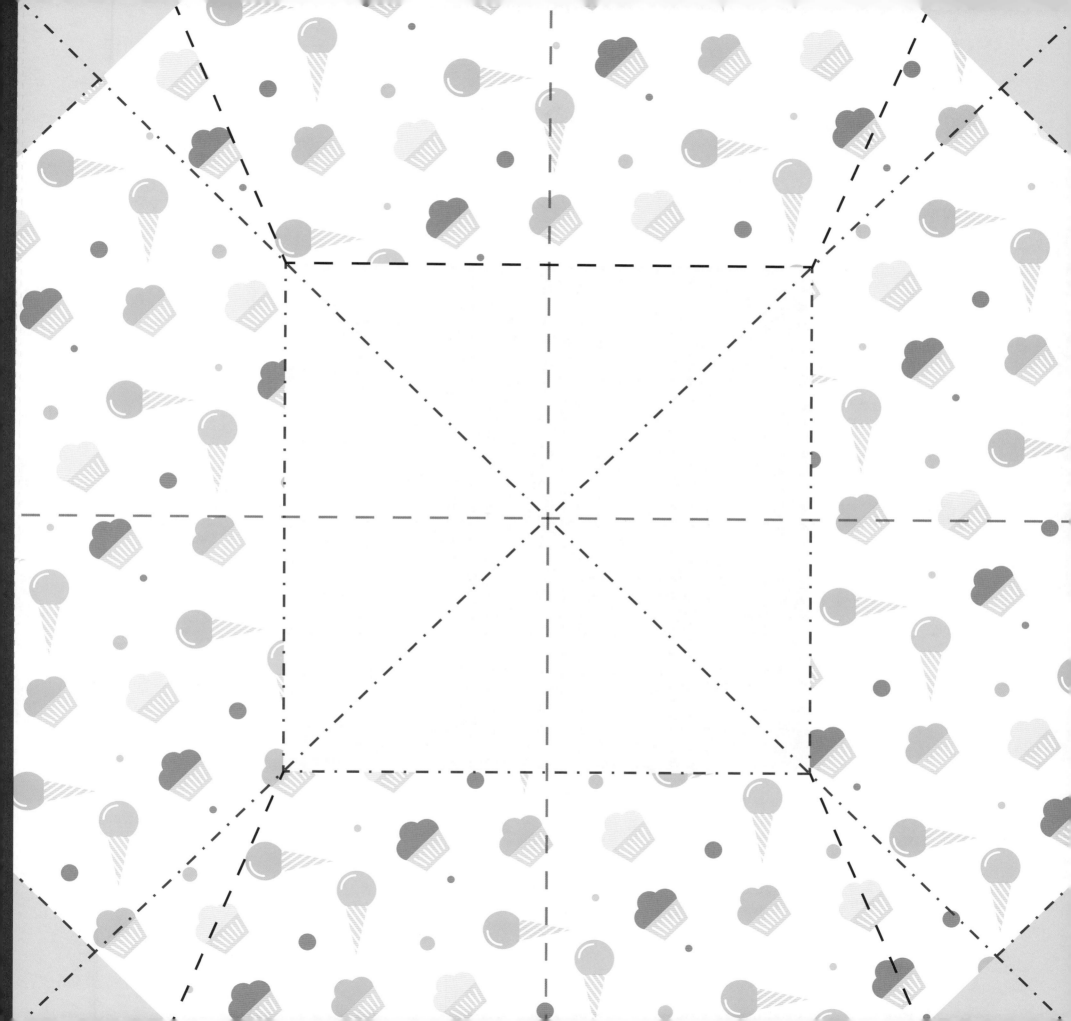

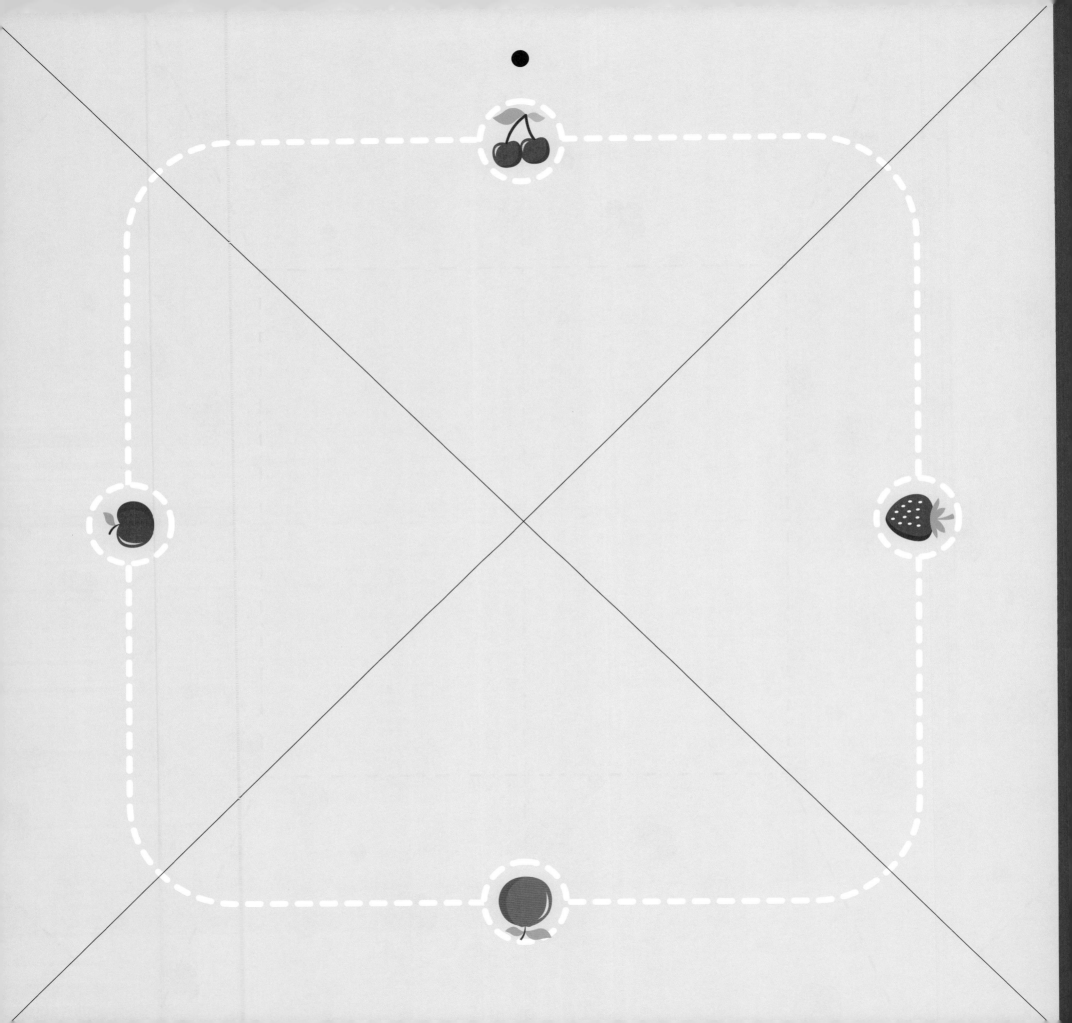

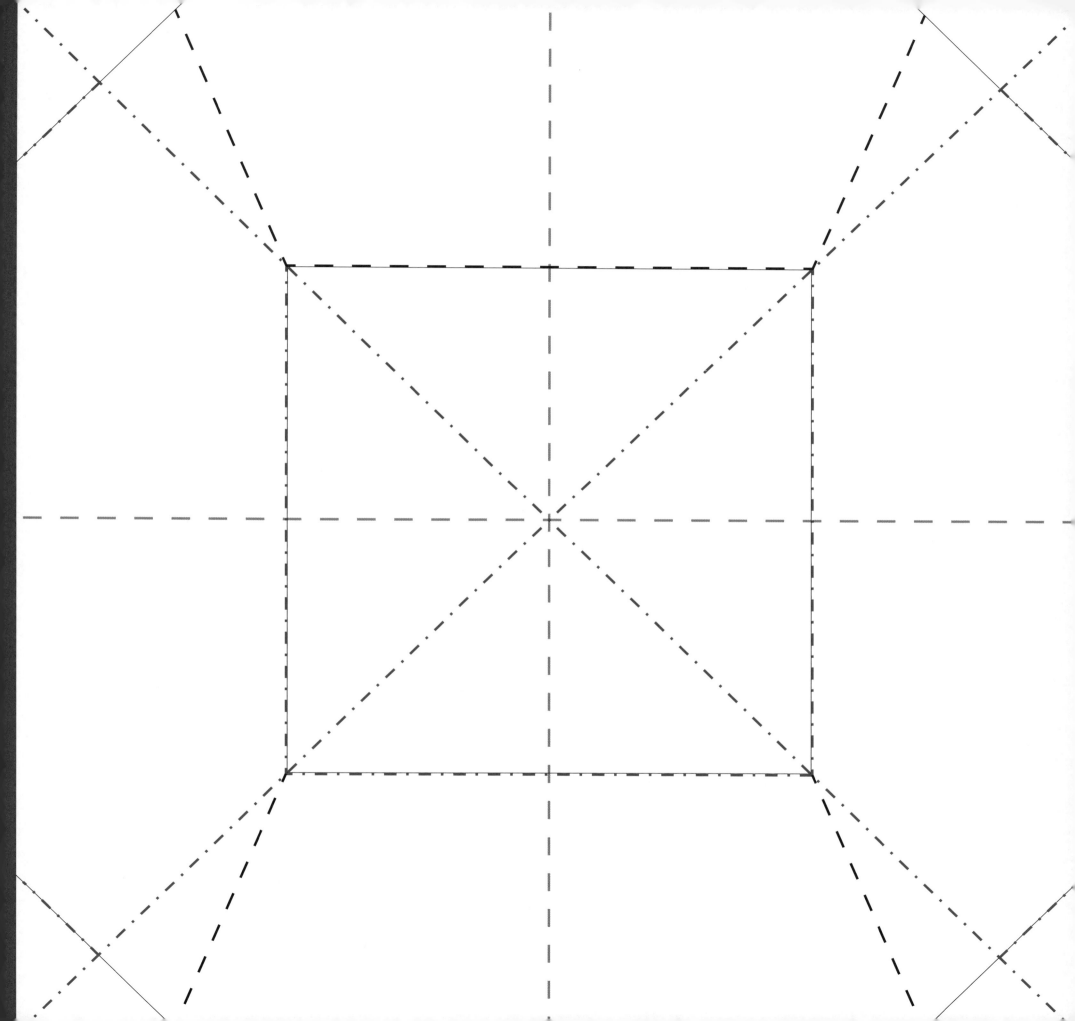

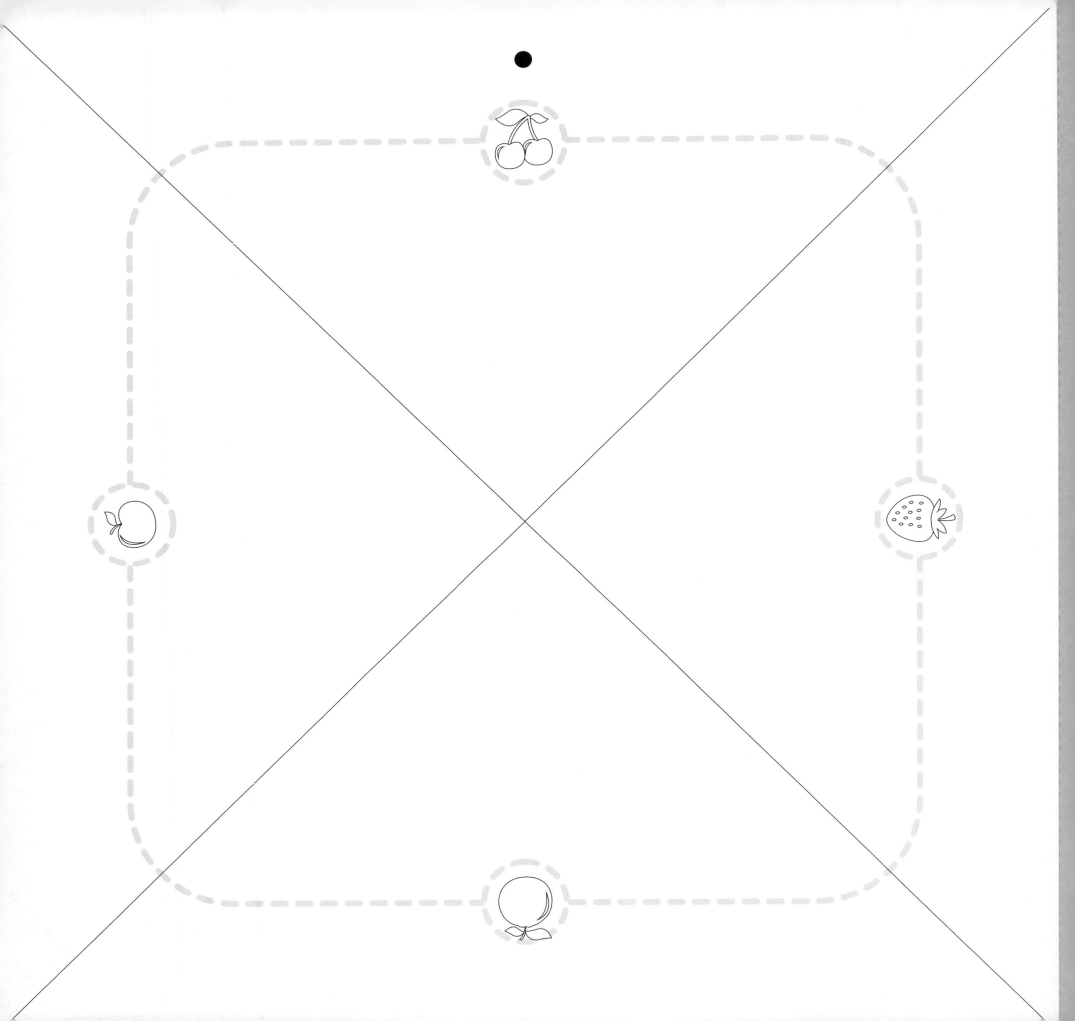

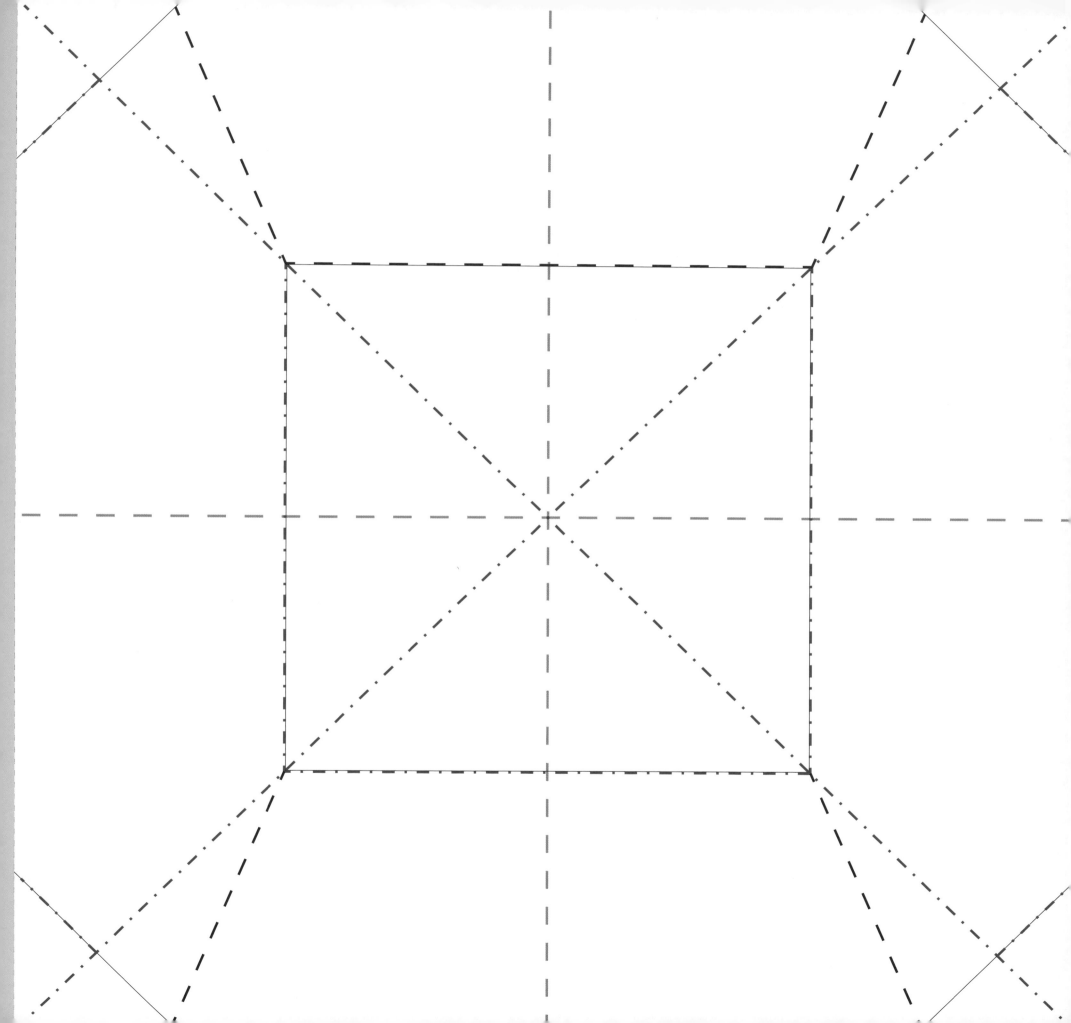

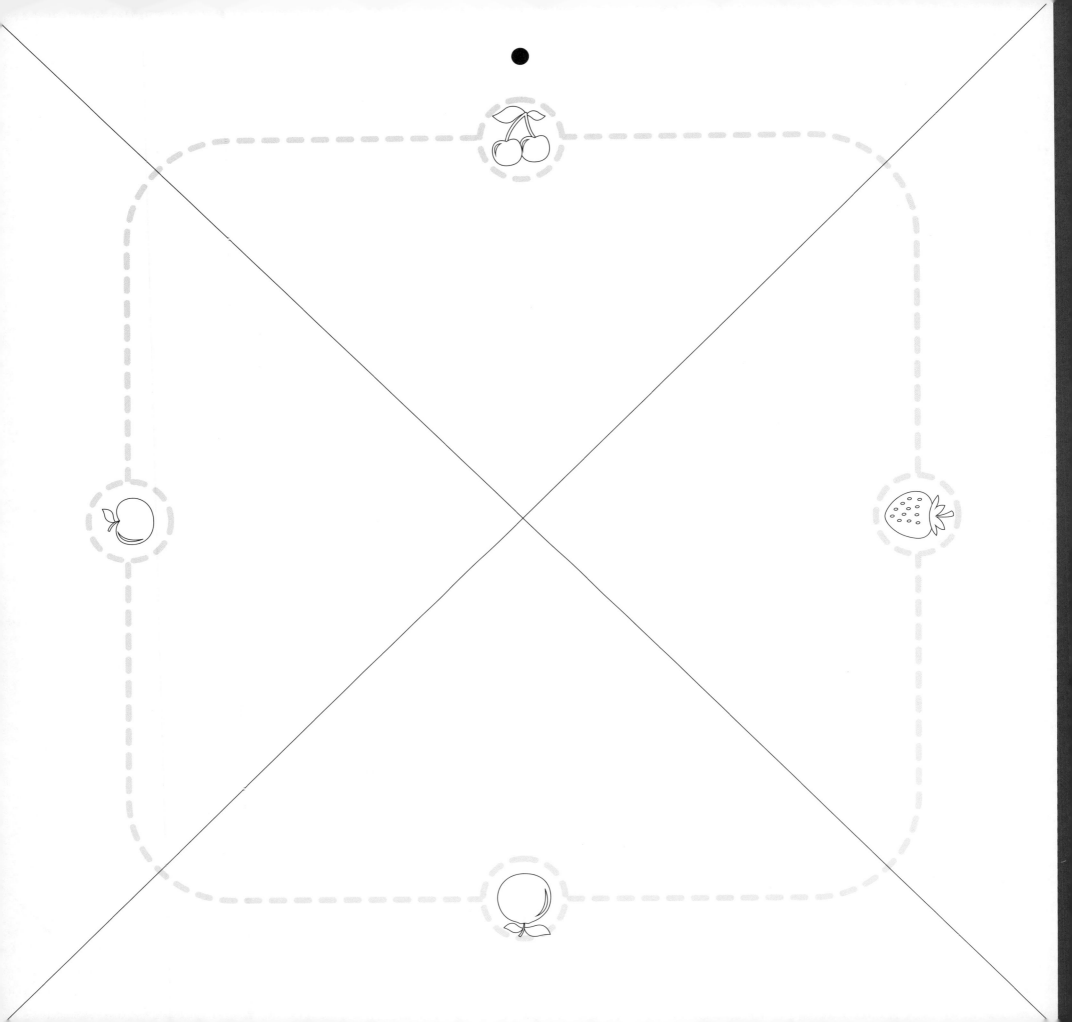

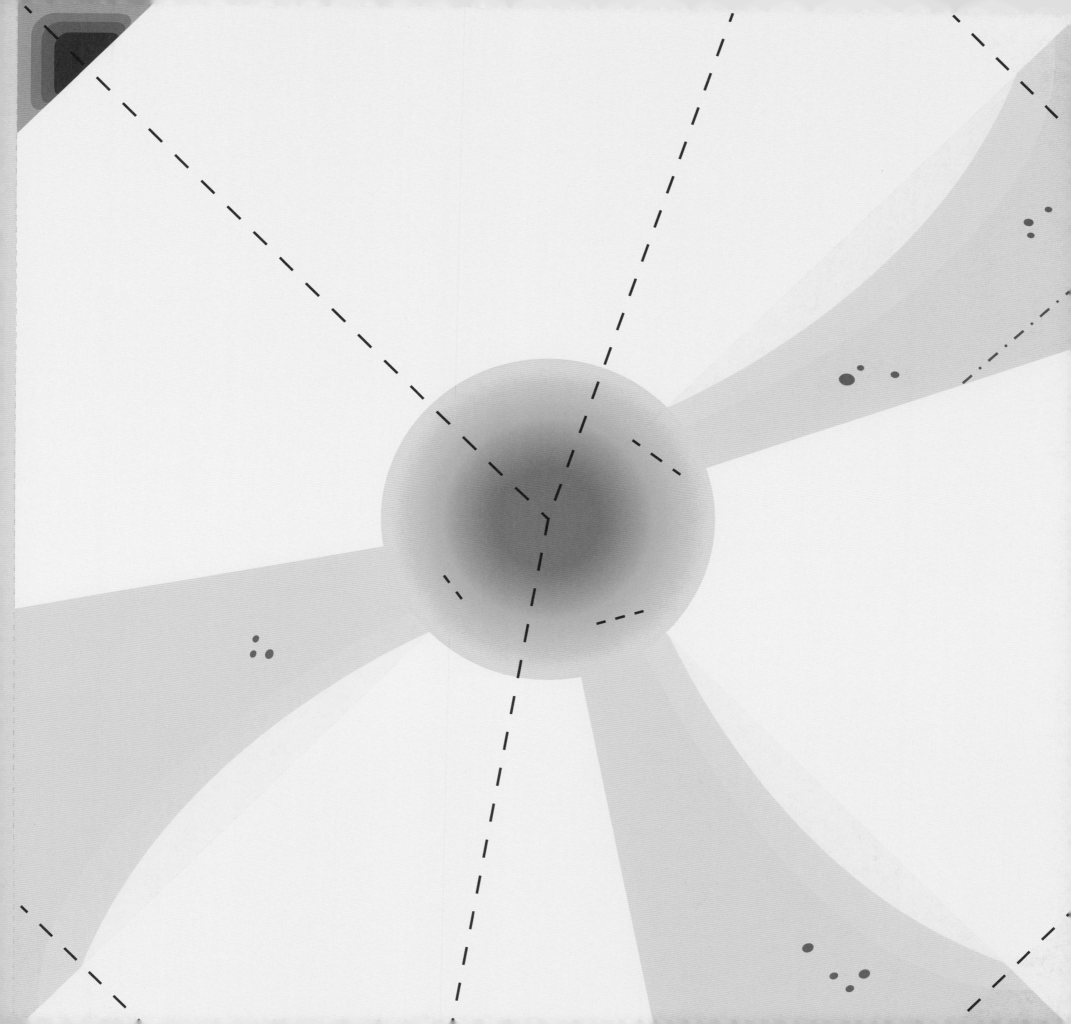

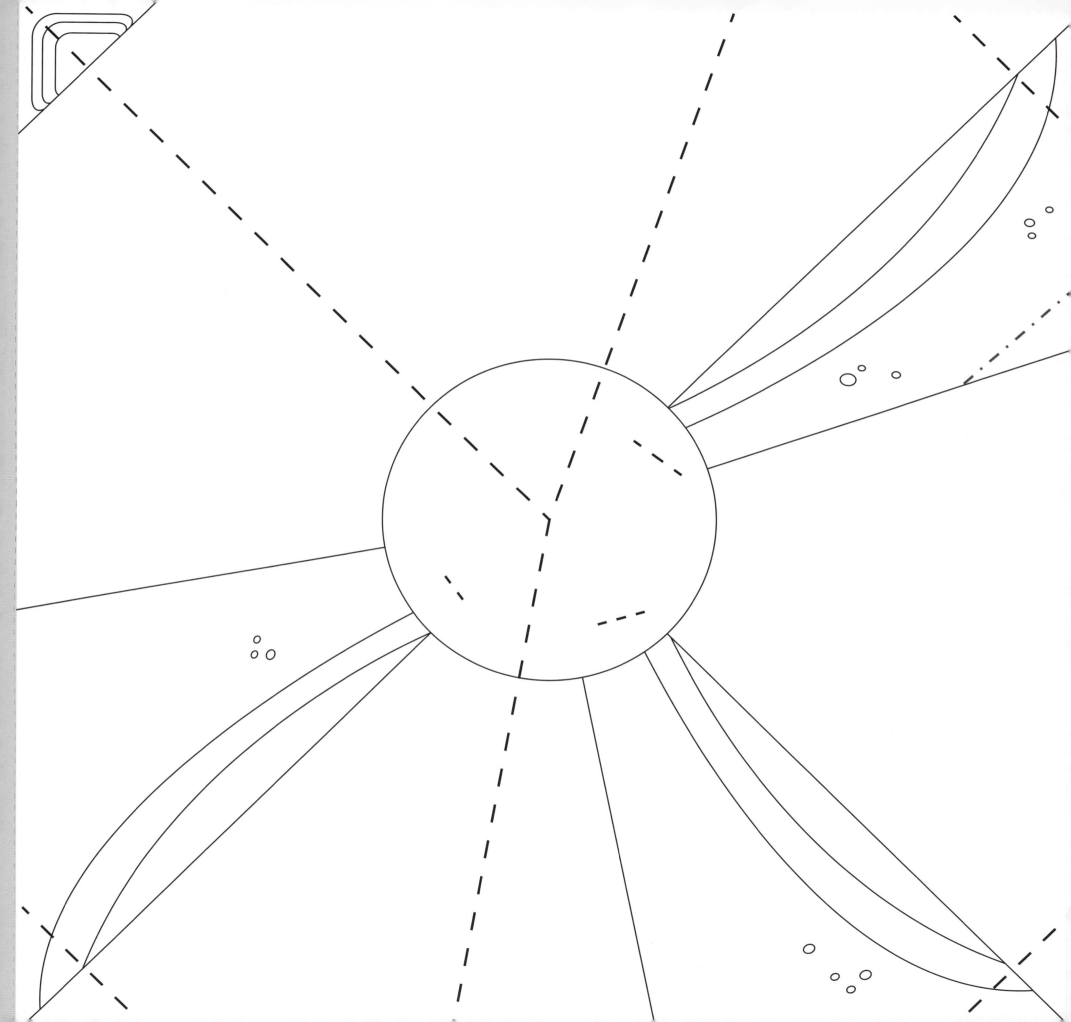

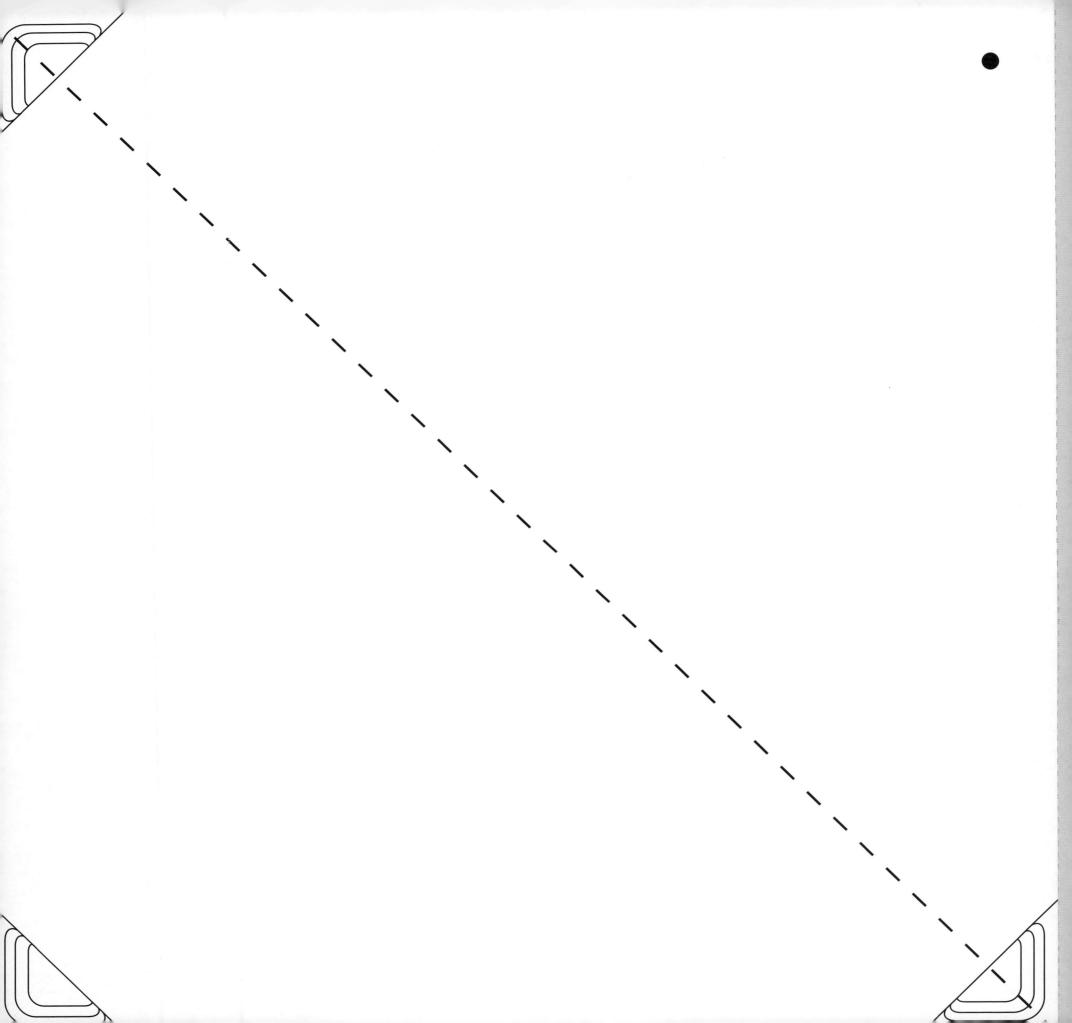

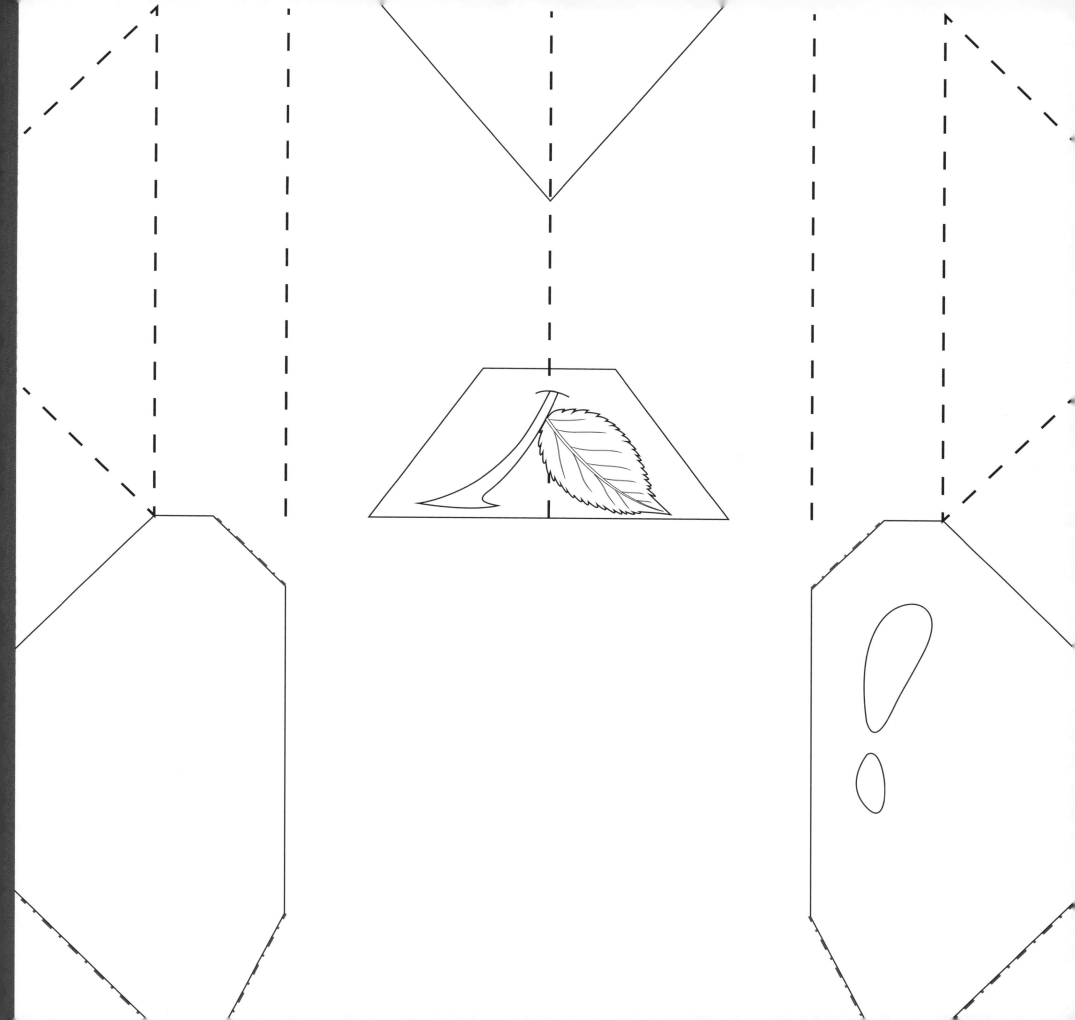

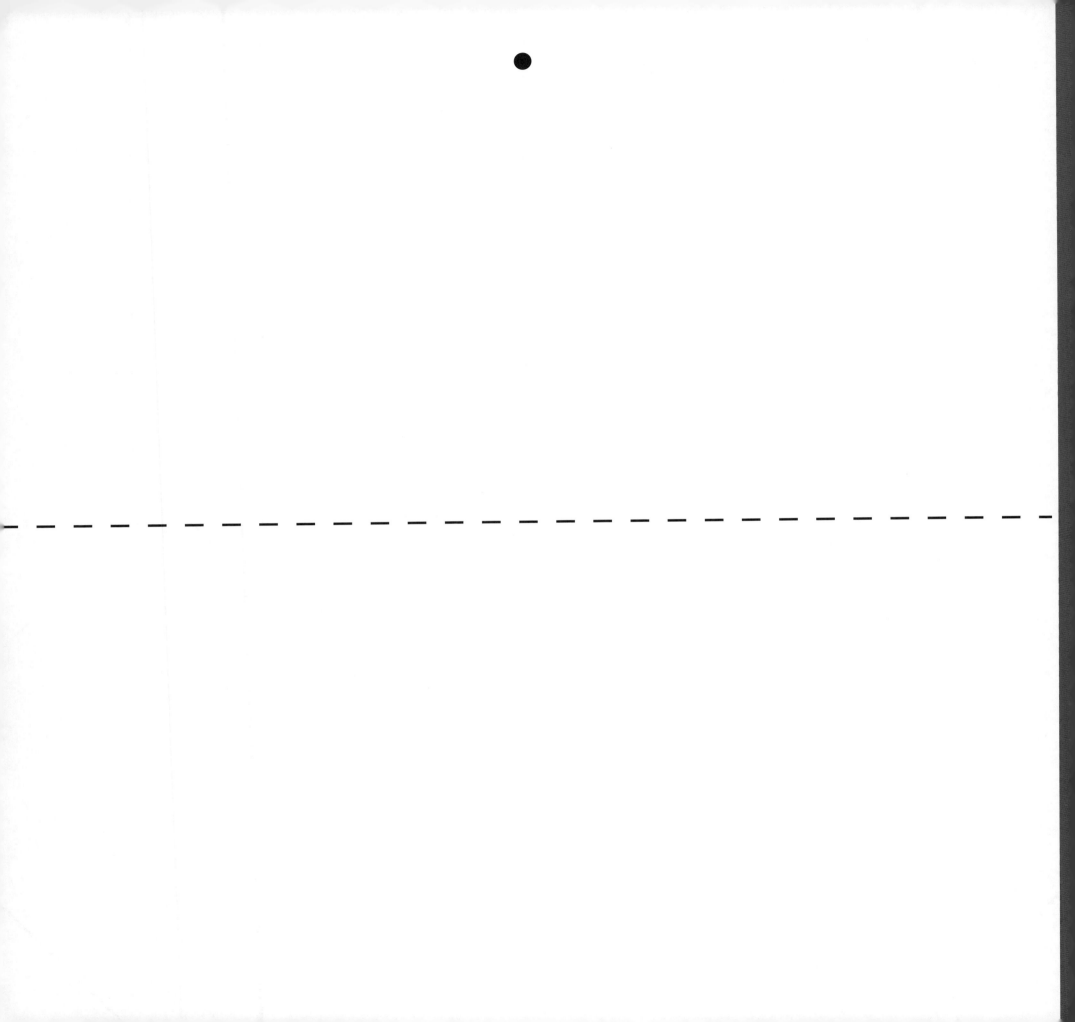

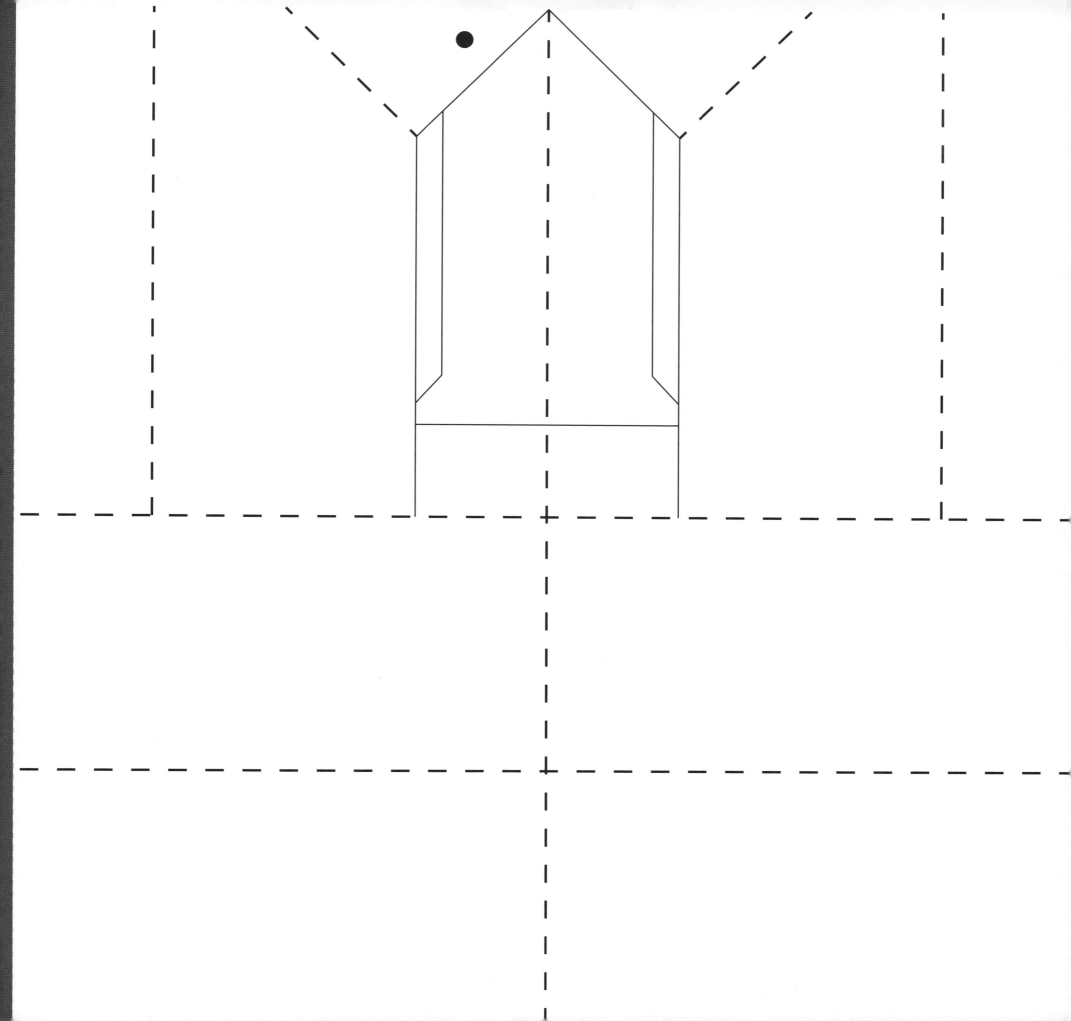

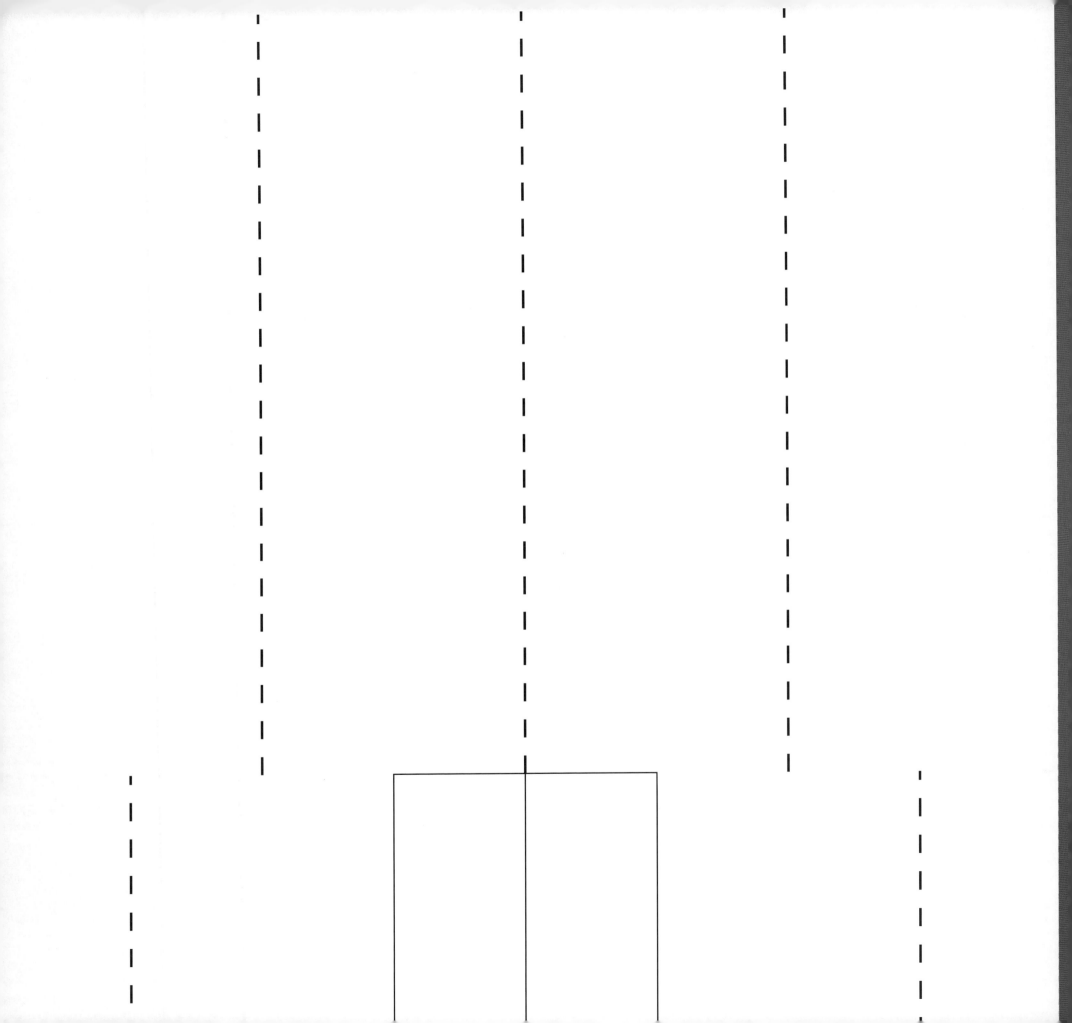

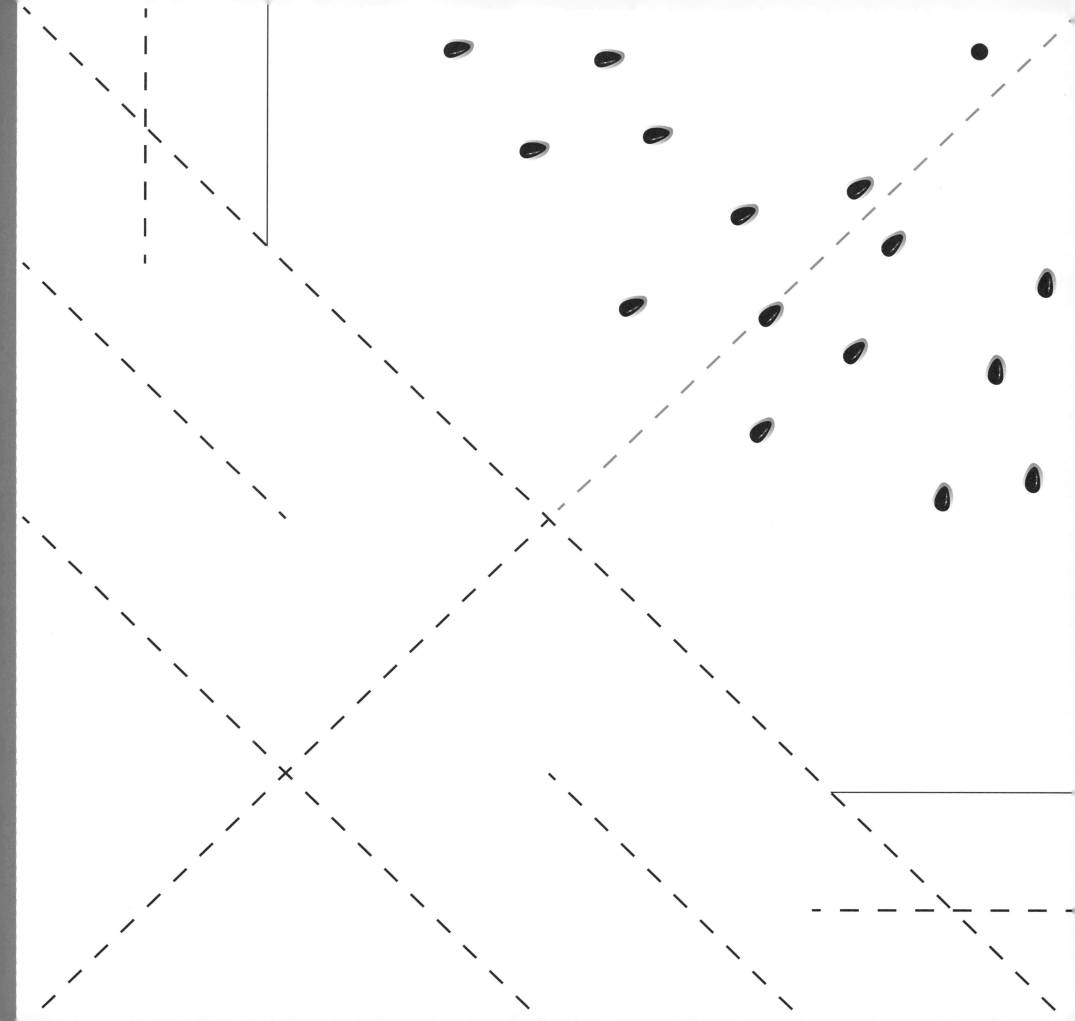

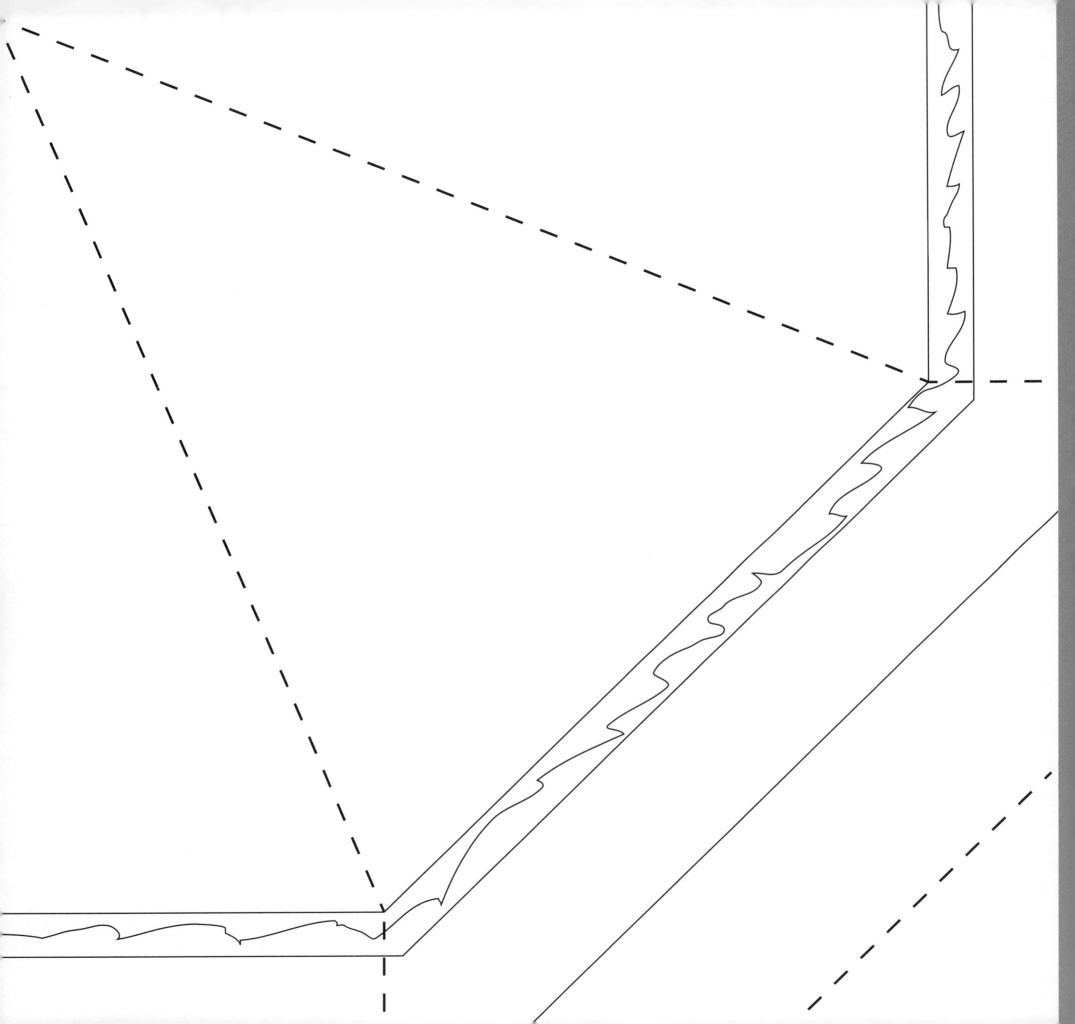

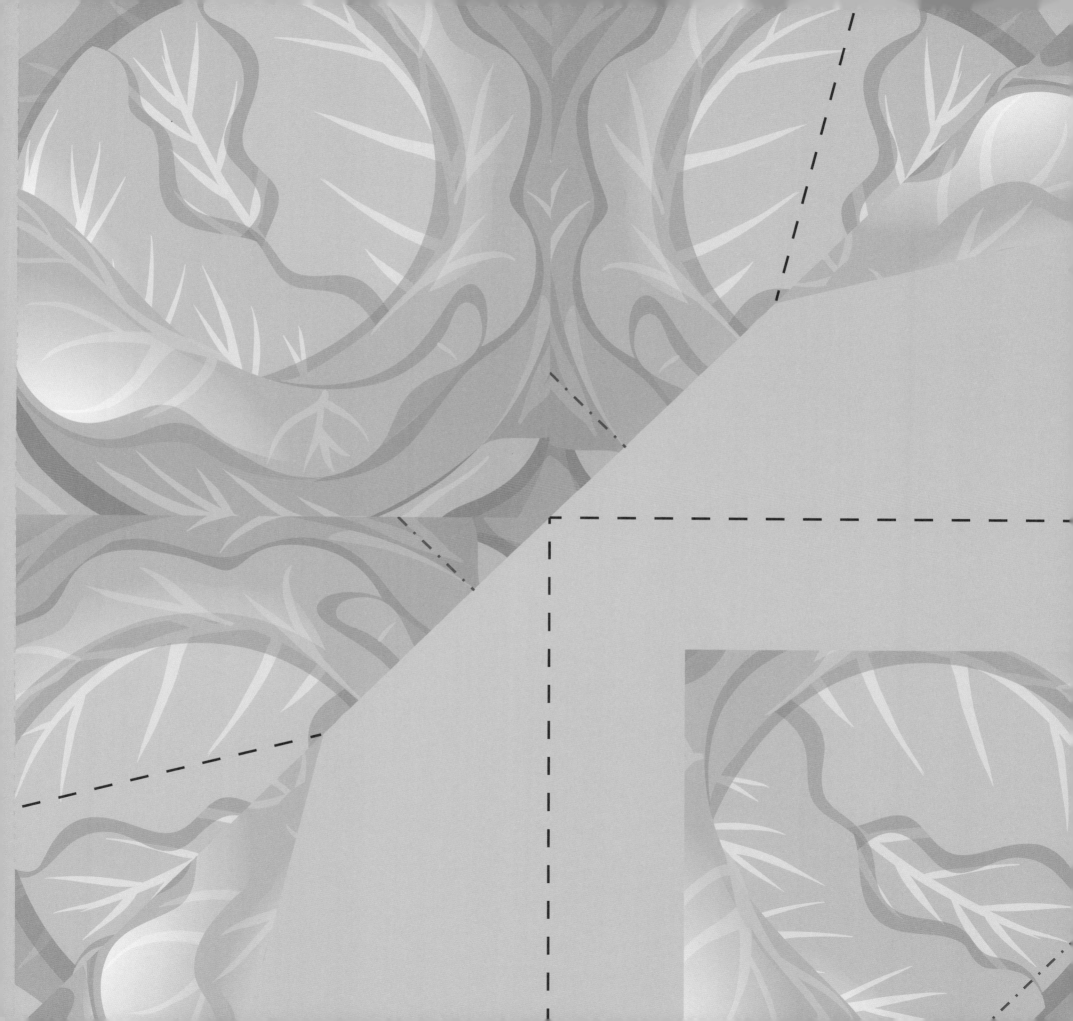

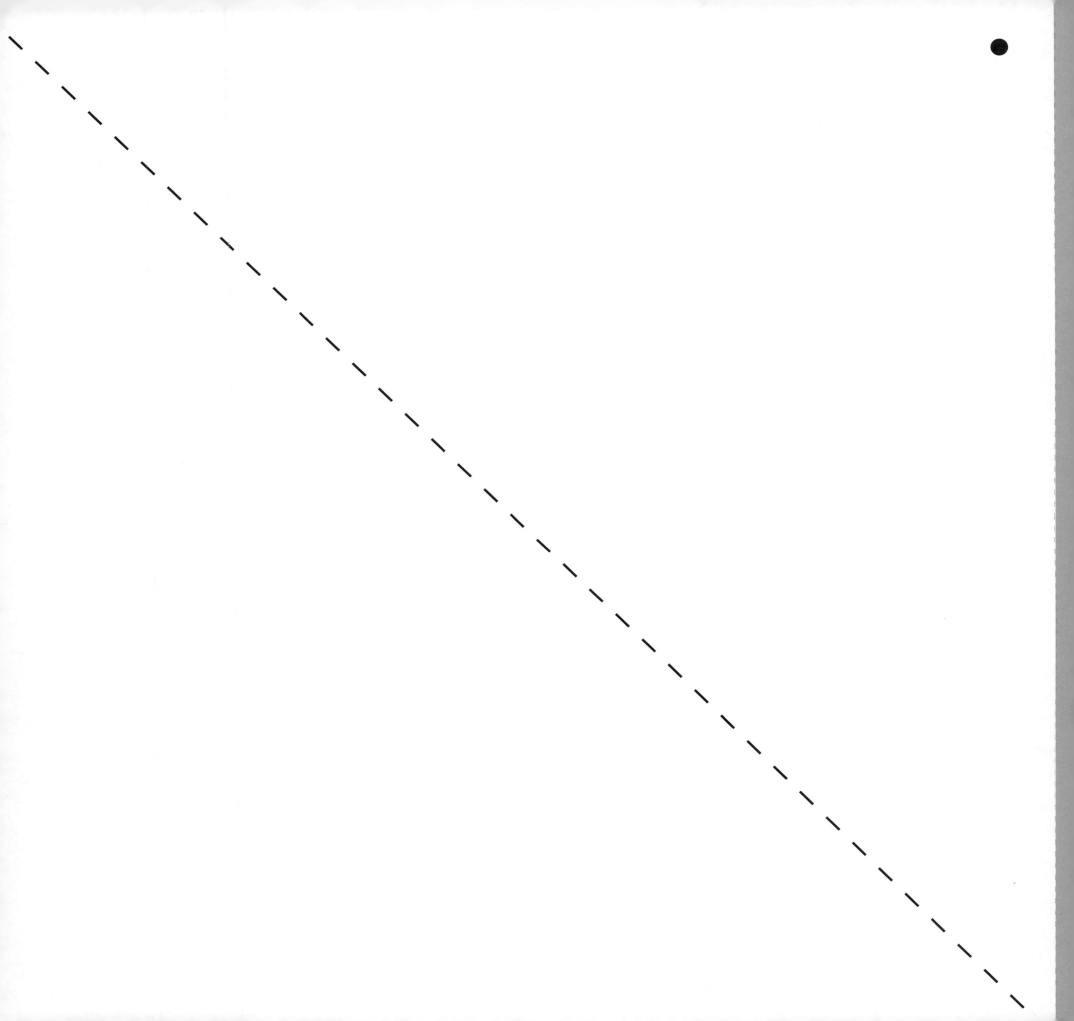

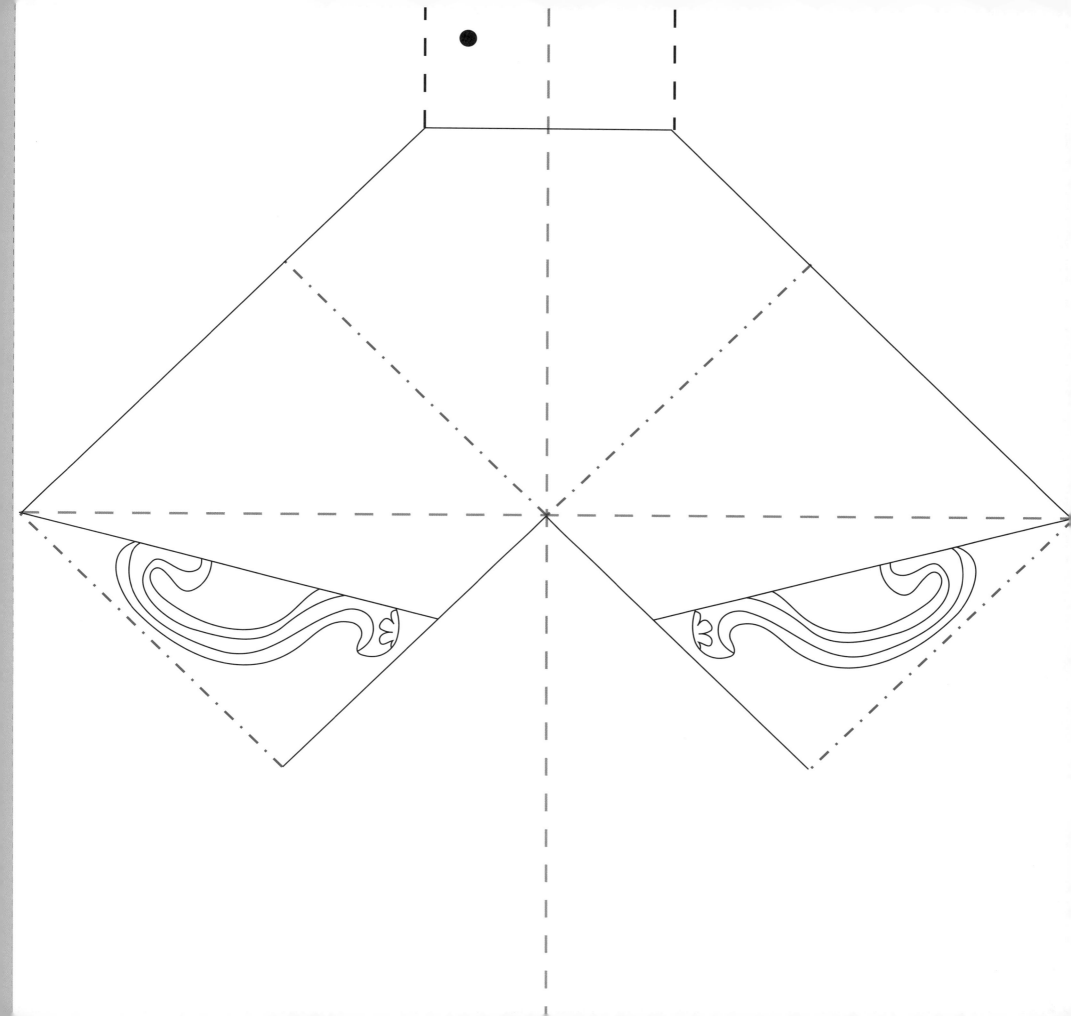

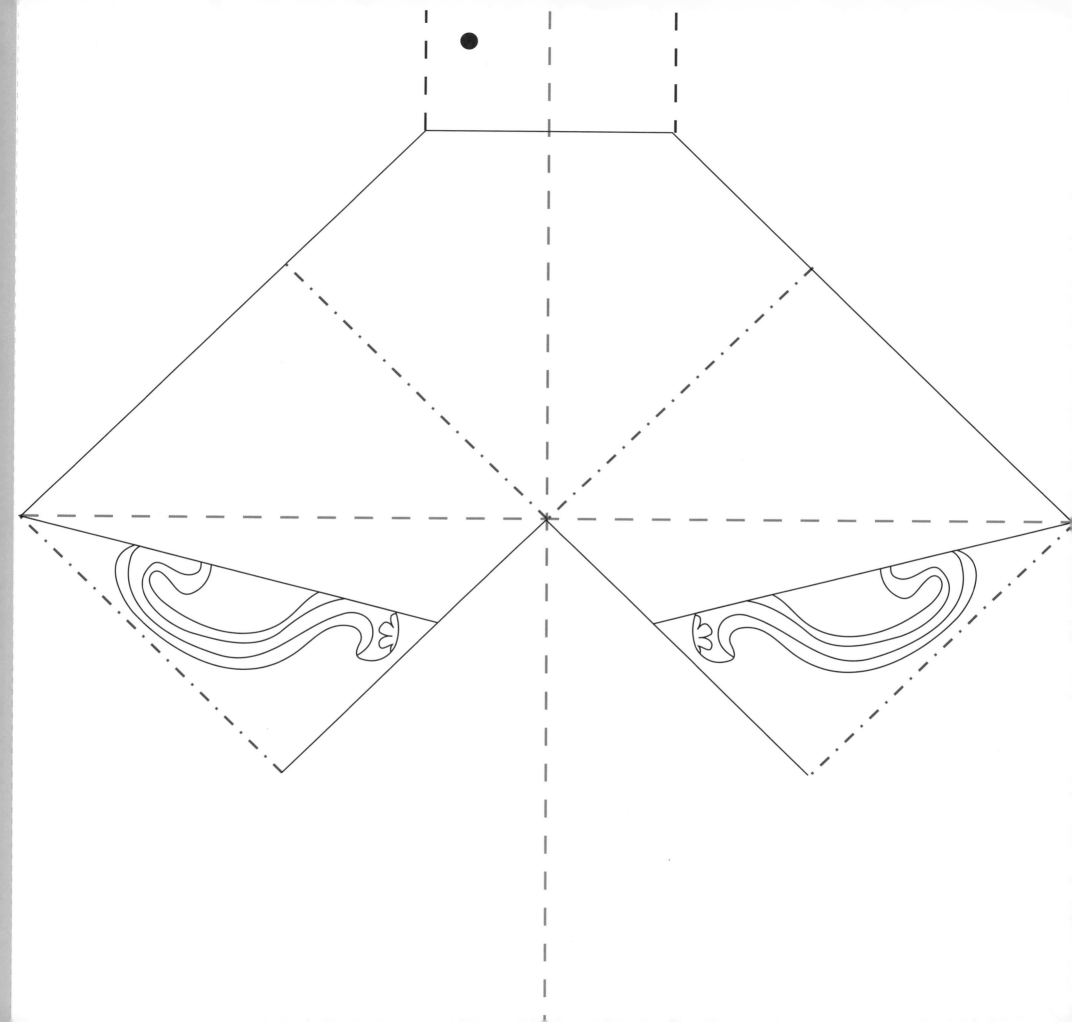